Seeking Asylum: Our Stories

Seeking Asylum

Our Stories

ASRC

Asylum Seeker
Resource Centre

Black Inc.

Published by Black Inc.,
an imprint of Schwartz Books
Level 1, 221 Drummond Street
Carlton VIC 3053, Australia
enquiries@blackincbooks.com
www.blackincbooks.com

9781760643300 (paperback)
978174382218 (ebook)

 A catalogue record for this
book is available from the
National Library of Australia

Design and typesetting by Tristan Main
Photography by Sam Biddle
Other photos courtesy of: Liliana Maria Sanchez Cornejo (p. 5);
Abdul Hekmat (p. 11); Danijel Malbasa (pp. 72–3); Barat Ali Batoor (pp. 84–5);
Tom Tran (top, p. 90); Thanush Selvarasa (pp. 120–3); Eamon Gallagher (p. 157).

Printed in Australia by Southern Impact.

Acknowledgement of Country

We would like to acknowledge and pay tribute to the first storytellers, the First Nations people of this land, who have been sharing stories for thousands of years, from generation to generation. Stories filled with teachings, culture, beliefs, values, dreaming and ways of life, stories which have endured through colonialism, genocide and discrimination. We honour and commit to continue to learn from the voices of past, present and emerging leaders of this land. May they continue to pave the way to a future where everyone has equal opportunity to belong, contribute and thrive in this country we call Australia.

Always was, always will be, Aboriginal land.

Contents

Nadira
50

Joseph
56

Rafique
60

Prudence
64

Danijel
68

Tenzin
74

Rahila
78

Batoor
82

Tom
88

Niro
92

Part One

Seeking Asylum

Liliana

Stories have power. By sharing our stories, we allow ourselves to be seen. In *Seeking Asylum*, twenty-three people with lived experience of seeking asylum share their stories with you.

Like them, my family sought asylum in Australia. I am the daughter of human rights activists; my father was a political prisoner. My family and I came to Australia as refugees on humanitarian visas. My name is Liliana Maria Sanchez Cornejo. I bear the names of both my grandmothers and the surnames of each of my parents. This connects me to my roots; it reminds me who I am and where I have come from.

I was born in Santiago, Chile, in 1983 – a dark moment in the country's history, when it was under the cruel dictatorship of Augusto Pinochet. Anyone who opposed him was imprisoned, tortured or made to disappear. Like those whose stories I am incredibly honoured to share with you in this book, *Seeking Asylum*, my family had to flee in search of safety.

Growing up in Australia, I was always the odd kid out in the classroom, as nobody knew where Chile was. When someone asked me where I came from, I would point to a map and say, 'That skinny country on the edge of Latin America.' I never shared the reasons why we had come here.

As an adult I found work with a refugee resettlement organisation. It was my dream job. From the first moment I researched the organisation, I knew that this was where I wanted to be, supporting people from a refugee background. My family and I were lucky to get an opportunity to start a new life and call Australia home, and I wanted to support other people like us. One day I was asked to share my story with a group of early learning educators. I was terrified, but I knew it was an opportunity to open up and share my experiences. I had wanted to do so for a long time, but I did not know how other people would react.

For the first time, I shared my history – my pain, my trauma – with strangers. I explained why my family had fled Chile and sought safety in a new country. I felt incredibly vulnerable. As I spoke, I relived the experience. Vivid memories surfaced: things from my childhood that I had long buried out of reach. Deep emotions overcame me and tears filled my eyes. When the session finished, I was shaking. I had mixed emotions. What had just happened?

But when I looked up, there were tears in other people's eyes as well. Some people in the audience came up to me afterwards and told me what an impact my story had had on them. Some admitted they didn't know much about refugees other than what they saw in the media. Others said their perceptions of people seeking asylum had shifted. Now they had a person to link to the abstract idea of seeking asylum – a person with a name and a face, hopes and fears, dreams and goals: a person just like them. By sharing my story, I had invited them to connect with me and they felt empathy as a result.

I realised that I was witnessing change happen right in front of my eyes. And that I was driving that change through story. This is how I learnt that the pain of the past is a tool that can change the narrative around seeking asylum.

As Chimamanda Ngozi Adichie has said, 'Telling only one story about a people or place creates stereotypes, and the problem with stereotypes is not that they are untrue, but that they are incomplete… When we reject the single story, when we realize there is never a single story about any place, we regain a kind of paradise.' Refugees are not a homogenous group. The people in this book may share one thing in common: seeking safety. But that's often where the similarities end. The ways they arrived here, how long it took to be granted a visa, whether they found the experience positive or incredibly damaging: all these things vary. And they also vary enormously in terms of who

they are beyond this experience. Seeking asylum is not the sum total of their identity. Sometimes even well-meaning discussion of refugees can create stereotypes. It's important that we do not expect people with lived experience to be either 'heroes' (contributing to society) or 'victims' (of traumas). People who have sought asylum just want to be seen and respected as human beings, and are just as diverse as any other group.

The global Ipsos survey carried out on World Refugee Day 2021 indicated that while most people support the right to seek refuge from war or persecution in principle, in practice people are reluctant to accept more refugees into their country. In Australia, the ongoing 'stop the boats' narrative, has contributed towards the 'more negative view towards refugees', according to Ipsos Australia director David Elliot.

By sharing our stories, we take back the narrative from those who do not have good intentions, those – such as some politicians and members of the media – who 'other' us, instil fear and use dehumanising rhetoric such as 'illegals', 'boat people' and 'coming to steal jobs'. Someone once said, 'borders are the scars of the earth'. Stories help to remove the borders that divide us. The differences we initially perceive when encountering 'the other' are shaped by our unconscious biases and by the dominant narrative we have heard.

Through telling our own stories, we have the opportunity to own the narrative about refugees and people seeking asylum. We are no longer a headline, a statistic or a slogan, but human beings.

We also raise our voices on behalf of those who do not have the opportunity to speak up: those who did not make it to safety. We speak for those still waiting to find out what the future holds for them – in refugee camps, detention centres or countries that do not grant them protection.

We build connection with others, break down barriers and take direct action against racism and discrimination.

The act of sharing one's story is one of generosity, requiring strength, courage and vulnerability. Through the stories in *Seeking Asylum*, the contributors take you on their journeys. Some of them are now physically safe but still unable to call this place home. Some of them are still separated from their families; some of them are in limbo, still in fear of being sent back to the very danger they have fled.

As a former refugee, my hope is that you listen to these words from author Khaled Hosseini: 'Refugees are mothers, fathers, sisters, brothers, children, with the same hopes and ambitions as us – except that a twist of fate has bound their lives to a global refugee crisis on an unprecedented scale.'

As an activist, I hope you recall James Baldwin's words: 'The world changes according to the way people see it, and if you alter, even by a millimeter, the way… people look at reality, then you can change it.'

And as an anthropologist, I hope you consider this: the differences we create between one another are a social construct, not based on science. Scientifically speaking, we all belong to one race, the human race.

In *Seeking Asylum*, I invite you to meet ordinary people who have escaped extraordinary circumstances.

Liliana Maria Sanchez Cornejo

Liliana Maria Sanchez Cornejo is a storyteller, cultural educator, anthropologist and activist. She is the founder of Moving Cultures Moving Stories, and is currently completing an Honours degree in anthropology, focusing on refugee stories as a tool to drive change.

Liliana

Abdul

Like other refugees, including those in this book, I am both a survivor and a witness.

As a child, I survived war and conflict in my home country, Afghanistan, often waking to gunshot fire during the civil war that broke out after the Soviet communist regime collapsed. I was internally displaced from a young age. In the 1990s, I survived the Taliban, who persecuted and massacred my people in Bamiyan, the Hazara heartland, and in Mazar-e-sharif. I then had a near-death experience during a five-day voyage to Australia: our boat's engine failed, leaving us stranded in the middle of the Indian Ocean, battling storms in the night. After Australia's navy found us, we were transferred to Darwin and then Curtin detention centre, in the middle of the Western Australian desert, where I spent months in despair, where I was stripped of my name, my identity – reduced to a number: 2671. Finally, in 2001, I was released on a Temporary Protection Visa.

A few months later, I was a witness to two events that dramatically changed Australia's refugee policies. First, a wooden fishing boat – carrying predominantly Hazara refugees fleeing the Taliban's brutality – became stranded in international waters north of Christmas Island. The boat's engine failed (just as our boat's had). The 438 people aboard were rescued by the Norwegian ship MV *Tampa*. The ensuing *Tampa* affair captured headlines in Australia and around the world. Following the rules of the sea, Captain Arne Rinnan of the *Tampa* headed for the nearest land, Christmas Island, but the Australian government refused to allow the *Tampa* to bring any of the refugees, many of whom were in very poor health, ashore. On the same day that SAS troops boarded the *Tampa* to prevent it from sailing closer to Christmas Island, Prime Minister John Howard tabled a Border Protection Bill that made such boardings legal and gave the Australian government sweeping powers to refuse entry to people seeking asylum by sea.

The refugees were taken to Nauru for processing, under the First Pacific Solution.

Just days later came the September 11 attacks on New York's World Trade Center and the Pentagon in Washington. In the aftermath, Australian politicians labelled us – refugees – potential terrorists. Tapping into a fear of asylum seekers, John Howard went on to win the 'unwinnable' election in November 2001.

Australia – indeed, the whole world – shifted after September 11. My world also changed radically in the wake of these two events. My younger brother had fled the Taliban and was supposed to follow me in seeking asylum in Australia, but he changed his plans when Australia closed its borders in the wake of *Tampa*. My brother travelled to Europe instead, where his odyssey ended – he was thrown into the water on the Greek coast, where he died. My visa did not allow me to leave the country, so I was unable to travel to Greece to find out what happened and get justice. I have been wracked with guilt ever since.

Life under Howard was traumatic, especially following the loss of my brother. I was grieving him and dealing with the uncertainty of my visa conditions, which did not allow me to travel or sponsor family members – just like the over 30,000 asylum seekers currently in Australia who can't bring their family members to Australia. The impact of those years left me with deep emotional wounds. However, I was unable to record the trauma that I and other refugees felt under Howard's government, as I did not have the language skills and was constrained by my status as a Temporary Protection Visa holder.

Over the years, I have witnessed Australia's preoccupation with refugees who arrive by boat. Fear and paranoia surround the idea of 'boat people', as if Australia will be overwhelmed by an influx of refugees. In reality, the number of people who arrive in Australia seeking asylum is a trickle compared to other countries. Turkey hosts more than 3.6 million Syrian refugees, Pakistan more than 1.4 million Afghan refugees and Iran more than 3 million

refugees, mostly from Afghanistan: the recent takeover of the country by the Taliban displaced thousands. We witnessed chaotic situations at Kabul airport as many sought to join millions of other Afghans in diaspora. The number of refugees in Australia is tiny in comparison. Under Howard, from 1999 to 2001, about 10,000 asylum seekers – 5000 a year – arrived by boat. These were mostly people who had fled Saddam Hussain in Iraq or the Taliban in Afghanistan. Under Labor's Kevin Rudd and Julia Gillard, 50,000 asylum seekers arrived by boat. Yet despite the small number – 10,000 asylum seekers a year – Australia implemented the strictest refugee policies in the world.

After the *Tampa* affair, Howard's government passed laws that became known as the 'Pacific Solution'. These included excising many of Australia's islands, including Christmas Island, from its migration zone, meaning asylum seekers had no automatic right to apply for refugee status if they arrived there.

A collective amnesia took hold during and after the First Pacific Solution. Very few testimonies of asylum seekers who were transferred from *Tampa* to Nauru appeared in the Australian media. The Australian public were not exposed to the cruelty of life on Nauru.

The stories and images of refugees were manipulated to achieve political outcomes. Sometimes this was as overt as politicians suggesting that asylum seekers deliberately threw children into the sea as a ploy to get rescued. Other times it was stealthier – our faces were hidden from the public and the government tightly controls who is able to tell our stories.

Despite the 'issue' of asylum seekers filling headline stories for years, the real stories of people seeking asylum have rarely been communicated. Asylum seekers are mostly presented as a mass of faceless people on rickety boats. They are incarcerated behind bars, either on the Australian mainland or in offshore centres, out of sight and out of mind. After *Tampa*, the Australian government instructed the navy not 'to humanise' asylum seekers. Without the public knowing the full story of horror and trauma people arriving by boat go through, it's hard for them to feel empathy and easy for doubts to be sowed in their minds. Thus refugees – especially those arriving by boat – remain blemished figures in the eyes of the Australian public.

It is hard for refugees to speak directly to the public and have their faces shown, because of government control. This starts at the border, continues in detention centres and extends even once they are in the community. For example, in 2014, when Scott Morrison was the immigration minister, he enacted a Code of Behaviour, which controlled the behaviour of asylum seekers released on bridging visas. Under this code, asylum seekers find it hard to speak to the media or tell their stories for fear of having their visa revoked or being back to detention centres.

Those who were sent to offshore centres under Howard's government, in the First Pacific Solution, remained hidden from the public view. A friend of mine, whom I parted ways within Indonesia, on the way to Australia, was sent to Nauru. I was not able to establish contact in 2001, before he was sent to Afghanistan. A decade later, he was resettled in Australia through the UNHCR program. He is retraumatised when he recalls the oven-like conditions on the inhospitable island, the despair and the ill-treatment by Australian authorities, who pressured refugees to return to their home countries as there was no hope for resettlement in Australia or anywhere else.

Given the ways the Australian government deters asylum seekers from raising their voices, witnessing is the only tool left for us to record and communicate our suffering and trauma to the sympathetic public. For the past decade I have brought refugee voices to the public through opinion pieces, journalism and art. I have recorded the testimonies of asylum seekers under the Coalition government for the past seven years. I feel a duty to do so, in order that this period in Australian history is never forgotten. For me, witnessing is a moral undertaking, as it is for refugees Behrooz Boochani and Abdul Aziz, who have spoken and written about imprisonment on Manus Island.

What I have witnessed over the past few years – the experiences of those asylum seekers who've shared their stories with me – is dehumanising and unspeakably horrific. The dehumanisation starts when asylum seekers arrive at a camp or centre – they are stripped of their identity and replaced with a number. Their capacity to engage with the outside world is severely restricted – for instance, access to phones and other means of communication is often tightly controlled. Some refugees on Nauru developed muteness in response – without words, they are even easier to control. Under the harsh conditions of the detention centre regime, brutality is the norm, and it can take asylum seekers a long time to be able to talk about their experiences – some are not able to speak at all because of trauma and how they have been dehumanised by the Australian immigration system. Thus, their capacity to bear witness has been diminished, if not extinguished.

Destroying asylum seekers' sense of self is at the heart of the ideology underpinning Australia's immigration detention system. Asylum seekers, some of whom experience extreme trauma in Australia's detention centre, have their personalities disintegrated, a dehumanising process that those held at Auschwitz experienced. In her book *The Origins of Totalitarianism*, Hannah Arendt explained how there are three stages of such disintegration: first, the destruction of the 'juridical person'; second, the destruction of the moral person through dehumanisation and by cutting them off from the outside world; and finally, the destruction of individuality and autonomy.

For four years, I spoke with a couple in Nauru who lived in a Kafkaesque situation. For a period of a month, they were medevacked to Australia after one of them descended into catatonia. Doctors from International Health and Medical Services (IHMS) and Nauru hospital refused to treat him in Nauru, so his partner was compelled to take the matter to court with the assistance of lawyers in Australia. The Australian government delayed their medical evacuation for weeks, leaving his partner in doubt whether he would be medevacked at all. It did not happen until the couple's lawyers took the matter to the Federal Court.

In 2017, I met another Hazara asylum seeker, who was injured in Nauru. His medical evacuation to Australia was delayed for weeks. He was transferred to Australia at the last minute. Doctors saved his life, but he lost his pancreas. At the hospital, he had two security guards by his bedside. He told me he was not allowed any visitors or to speak with his family for six months. By the time he was released, he had almost lost his sanity and was at breaking point. 'I want to jump from the bridge,' he told me.

For the past two decades refugees have been labelled 'boat people' or 'queue jumpers' – and treated as a burden. Our presence has preoccupied the whole nation, but our stories have been excluded from the national narrative. Politicians have often capitalised on deaths at sea for political gain rather than make the public aware of the trauma refugees endure coming by boat. Over thirty asylum seekers have taken their lives in Australia in the past six years. The impact of their deaths has reverberated not only through their families but also the wider community, leaving a whole generation of refugees traumatised. Even the suicides and self-immolations of asylum seekers hasn't sufficiently alarmed the public to change the policies that inflict such irreparable wounds on refugees.

July 2021 marked eight years since the Second Pacific Solution was introduced by Rudd's government. In 2008, he abolished the First Pacific Solution. Five years later, he resurrected it, declaring that 'asylum seekers who come here by boat without a visa will never be settled in Australia'.

Under the Second Pacific Solution, information about the life of asylum seekers offshore has been severely controlled. Many refugees have gone through extreme trauma – trauma so bad that some children descended into catatonia and had to be medevacked.

Today, the Australian government continues to keep 30,000 asylum seekers in legal limbo without being able to sponsor their families, be eligible for settlement services or have the right to education unless they enrol as international fee-paying students. They have been separated from their families for eight years and many live in the quagmire of despair. Most have pernicious depression and trauma as a result of their experiences in detention centres or on bridging visas. One vulnerable group are my people, the Hazaras, who in August 2021 watched the sudden takeover of Afghanistan by the Taliban. Again, the Taliban massacred Hazaras – this time in Malistan, a district of Ghazni province, according to an Amnesty International report on 20 August 2021.

Many of us live with wounded memories, as much from what we have experienced in Australia as from what we lived through back home. 'All wars are fought twice,' Viet Thanh Nguyen, the Pulitzer Prize–winning author of *The Sympathizer*, writes, 'the first time on the battlefield, the second time in memory.' Refugees, of course, carry trauma from our home countries due to war and conflict, but the real battlefield for many of us who arrive by boat is the Australian political landscape. We fight to survive Australia's cruel policies, endure long periods in detention, including being kept in gulag-like conditions in Nauru, and live apart from our families for years. Strict censorship laws mean anyone who leaks information can be punished. In 2015, the Australian government legislated the Border Force Act, which meant that anyone who leaked information from offshore centres could face up to two years' imprisonment. Through the power of witnessing, we are able to break the system of control: I obtained video footage of refugees from Nauru in 2017 and showed it at an exhibition called 'The Invisible', held at UTS gallery in Sydney. It showed the human faces behind the myths.

The cruel Australian policies have cost too many lives in the past eight years; fourteen refugees and asylum seekers have died in the offshore detention system, including Reza Barrati who was killed on Manus Island. Over twelve asylum seekers have died in the community, most on bridging visas. I have been close to many of these cases, as I reported on them. One was Khodayar Amini, a Hazara asylum seeker, who self-immolated in October 2015 after the Australian Border Force raided his home in Sydney to re-detain him. Two months later, another asylum seeker, Mohammad Nazeri, hanged himself on a construction site in Western Sydney because he could not be reunited with his family – asylum seekers are barred from sponsoring family members. In June 2015, a 22-year-old asylum seeker, Mohammad Hadi, hanged himself in a park close to my home in Western Sydney. Hadi was an intelligent guy, an avid reader, who read the poetry of Hafiz, Rumi and Saidi to deal with his despair on a bridging visa – but poetry did not save him. Hadi had been studying at a university in Afghanistan; he fled after his classmate was killed by the Taliban. He arrived in Australia in 2012 and was released on a bridging visa. He wished to pursue his studies but his visa conditions didn't allow him to study or work. He spent most days at home and plunged into a deep depression from which he never recovered. Six Hazara asylum seekers took their lives in just two

Nimat, a Hazara asylum seeker, places flowers on his brother Hadi's grave, June 2015.

years; it increasingly became part of our daily life, a subject of everyday discussion in the community and at home.

For a long time, refugees in Australia have not been in charge of telling their stories because their capacity to bear witness has been severely restricted. Kurdish-Iranian journalist Behrouz Boochani, who was detained on Manus Island for four years, resisted the system by bearing witness to the cruelty of the Manus detention centre. His prize-winning memoir, *No Friend But the Mountains*, was tapped out on a mobile phone in a series of single messages over time. But Boochani's case is a rare exception. It has been far more common for others – academics, journalists and artists, who do not have lived experience of seeking asylum – to speak on their behalf.

The discourse around seeking asylum will only change when refugees are able to tell their stories themselves.

Seeking Asylum brings these hidden voices to the surface. For too long in this country the stories of refugees and asylum seekers have been told through the prism of the white gaze. In *Seeking Asylum*, refugees show their faces and tell their own stories in their own words.

Abdul Karim Hekmat

Abdul Hekmat is a writer, journalist and photographer. His photography exhibition, *Unsafe Haven*, toured nationally and was shown in prestigious galleries around Australia. His curated exhibition, *The Invisible*, won the UTS Human Rights Award in 2018. Abdul has written for *The Guardian*, *The Saturday Paper*, *The Sydney Morning Herald*, *The Age* and *The Monthly*. He was a finalist for the 2018 Walkley Freelance Journalist of the Year, and for the United Nations Media Peace Prize and Amnesty Media Prize in 2016. He graduated with honours in a BA Communications (social inquiry) at UTS in 2009. In 2012, he was awarded Alumni Award for his work with refugees. Now, he is a PhD candidate at the University of Technology, Sydney (UTS), where he explores the experiences, trauma and memories of asylum seekers and refugees in Australia.

Understanding the Injustices

Julian Burnside AO QC, with Jana Favero

Who can seek asylum?

Everyone has the right to seek asylum.

This right is inscribed in the Universal Declaration of Human Rights (UDHR), an international document adopted by the United Nations, which lays out the rights and freedoms of all human beings. Article 14 of the UDHR provides:

Everyone has the right to seek and to enjoy in other countries asylum from persecution.

Australia played a role in the creation of the UDHR far greater than our then population of 7 million would have suggested. When the UDHR was endorsed by the United Nations on 10 December 1948, an Australian, H.V. 'Doc' Evatt, presided over the UN General Assembly.

It is a fundamental human right to seek asylum – not a crime – and people should be welcomed and supported when they arrive in Australia asking for our protection.

Instead, Australia's treatment in recent years of people seeking asylum suggests that we have no respect for this fundamental human right, or the UDHR, and that we lack compassion for people who have fled their homes in fear for their lives.

A brief chronology

1948   The Universal Declaration of Human Rights is adopted by the UN

1954   Australia signs the Refugee Convention

1976   The first people seeking asylum by boat arrive in Australia from Vietnam, and Australia begins to take thousands of refugees from Vietnam

1977   Prime Minister Malcolm Fraser introduces Australia's Humanitarian Program

1989   Prime Minister Bob Hawke announces an additional 42,000 places for Chinese refugees in response to Tiananmen Square

1992   Australia's *Migration Act* is amended to provide for mandatory immigration detention

1999   Prime Minister John Howard introduces Temporary Protection Visas

2001   Under John Howard, after the MV *Tampa* incident, Australia sends first people to Nauru, the Pacific Solution is formed and offshore processing commences

2005   Community Detention is introduced

2007   Under Prime Minister Kevin Rudd, offshore processing ceases

2008   Temporary Protection Visas are abolished

2010   High Court decision ('M61') allows people seeking asylum access to Australian courts for judicial review, regardless of place or means of arrival

       Christmas Island boat disaster, resulting in the death of fifty-two people seeking asylum

2012   Under Prime Minister Julia Gillard, offshore processing reopens and first people sent to Nauru

2013   Under Kevin Rudd, Papua New Guinea (PNG) solution announced

2014   Under Prime Minister Tony Abbott and Immigration Minister Scott Morrison, the *Migration Act* is amended, the 'legacy caseload', which removes most references to the Refugee Convention in the *Migration Act*, reintroduces Temporary Protection Visas and Fast Track processing, introducing an unfair and prolonged refugee determination system (despite the name!)

2015   Tony Abbott announces additional 12,000 humanitarian places for Syrian refugees

2018   Under Prime Minister Scott Morrison, Medevac legislation is passed allowing refugees to be transferred to Australia from PNG/Nauru – it is the first time since 1929 that a sitting government has lost a vote in the House of Representatives

2019   Scott Morrison wins the federal election and Medevac is repealed

2021   Further changes are made to the *Migration Act*, meaning that the indefinite detention of refugees is enshrined in law by the federal parliament

What is the difference between a refugee and a person seeking asylum?

Refugees are defined and protected in international law. The 1951 Convention and Protocol Relating to the Status of Refugees – also known as the Refugee Convention – defines a refugee as a person who:

> owing to well-founded fear of being persecuted for reasons of race, religion, nationality, membership of a particular social group or political opinion, is outside the country of his nationality and is unable, or owing to such fear, is unwilling to avail himself of the protection of that country; or who, not having a nationality and being outside the country of his former habitual residence as a result of such events, is unable or, owing to such fear, is unwilling to return to it.

> A person who flees their country and seeks protection in another country is known to be 'seeking asylum'. If their claim for asylum is accepted, they then become a refugee.

PERSON SEEKING ASYLUM Someone who flees their country due to fears of persecution, or because they have experienced violence or human rights violations, and seeks protection in another country. They are classified as an **asylum seeker** until their claim for protection has been established (by meeting strict criteria through a Refugee Status Determination Process).

REFUGEE Someone who has fled their country and whose claim for asylum has been accepted. They may have been resettled in another country or are awaiting resettlement.

Seeking asylum is a point in someone's life. People seeking asylum are neighbours, brothers, sisters, parents, doctors, teachers, engineers – who have to flee in order to escape persecution. Seeking asylum shouldn't define who they are, but that's what we do in Australia through the creation of a punitive system that fails people who are seeking safety and protection.

Even when a person who is seeking asylum in Australia is found to be a refugee, the outcome is different to anywhere else in the world. Changes made to Australian law in 2014 mean some refugees are only granted a Temporary Protection Visa (TPV) or Safe Haven Enterprise Visa (SHEV). Others who are found to be refugees but arrived by boat – *without a visa* – will never be granted protection in Australia because of how they came here. These people are subject to offshore processing. Further changes made to the *Migration Act* in 2021 mean, in principle, that refugees could remain in detention forever if a person is refused a visa (or their visa is cancelled) on character grounds. This arguably involves Australia in a crime against humanity, as a matter of international law. In fact, much of what Australia does is in direct conflict with international law, but our courts only give effect to local Australian law.

What is the process for seeking asylum?

The answer to this question could form a book in itself (and many excellent scholars, lawyers and academics have written books on this topic). In the simplest terms, someone who is seeking asylum goes through a Refugee Status Determination process to assess if they meet one of the five criteria of being a refugee.

The Refugee Convention (1951), which Australia signed in 1954, defines a refugee as follows:

> someone who is unable or unwilling to return to their country of origin owing to a well-founded fear of being persecuted for reasons of race, religion, nationality, membership of a particular social group, or political opinion.'

Australia approaches the Refugee Status Determination process in a different way to the rest of the world. In Australia, the process varies depending on how and when you arrived seeking asylum. The main difference is whether people arrive with a valid visa or not (generally those without a visa arrive by boat).

1. Arrival with a visa
(such as student, business, visitor visa)

People with an official visa – such as a student, sports, business or tourism visa – arrive in Australia via aeroplane and can apply for asylum during their visit. While their application for asylum is being dealt with, they are allowed to live in the community, and most Australians are blissfully unaware of their presence in Australia.

2. Without a visa (arrival by boat)

Those who cannot get a visa are left with no option but to find other ways to safety, typically via boat. They are placed in detention – or, since 2013, sent automatically to Manus Island (Papua New Guinea) or Nauru for offshore processing. In the vast majority of these cases, people are successful in their claims for protection but will never be settled in Australia because they came without a visa and are effectively punished for their mode of arrival, contrary to the Refugee Convention.

In Australia, unlike the rest of the world, even when someone meets the criteria and is assessed as a refugee, we only offer temporary protection if they arrived by boat after 2013. That is, people have to keep proving they are a refugee and reapplying for temporary protection. This goes against the principles enshrined in the Refugee Convention (which Australia helped draft and which we were an early signatory of) and it took a law change in 2014 to make temporary protection a reality for those seeking asylum. Thanks to this change, some refugees will be granted a Temporary Protection Visa (TPV) or Safe Haven Enterprise Visa (SHEV).

People without a visa must be put in detention and remain in detention until they receive a visa or are removed from Australia. But another change to the *Migration Act* in mid-2021 means that the Minister for Immigration can revoke or refuse a visa on character grounds. This change makes it unnecessary to remove such a person from Australia, meaning refugees in detention could be detained indefinitely.

The process of seeking refugee status is, to say the least, patchy.

An example: a person seeking asylum arrived in Australia by boat late in 2013. Because offshore processing was mandatory, he was sent to Manus Island (PNG). The PNG authorities quickly assessed him as a refugee, but he remained in detention for another six years. He developed a cardiac problem, which the PNG system could not deal with. He was brought to Australia, *by the Australian government*, under the Medevac legislation, which allowed sick refugees to be transported to Australia for treatment on the advice of doctors (that legislation was repealed by the Morrison government). Australia put him in detention, and he stayed about a year in detention until he was sent to the United States under the US deal. He *never got the cardiac treatment* he was brought to Australia for! This is an example of how discretionary considerations operate to the detriment of people who came here by boat.

Leave aside that the *Migration Act* is complex, there are many discretions in it which seem to be determined, uniformly, against the interests of 'boat people'. When the Tamil family from Biloela, Queensland, were moved from Christmas Island to Perth in June 2021, the immigration minister, Alex Hawke, issued a press release. It included this:

The Government's position on border protection has not changed. Anyone who arrives in Australia illegally by boat will not be resettled permanently.

That press release simply repeats the lie on which the mistreatment has flourished: that people who come here by boat, seeking asylum, are in some way criminals.

How did Australia's asylum policy go so wrong?

Australia's mistreatment of people arriving in Australia by boat to seek asylum began with a legislative change in 1992, when the *Migration Act* was amended so as to identify, specifically, a group who were non-citizens *without a visa*.

Years later, the *Tampa* case resulted in a hardening of Australia's treatment of those people. The *Tampa* case was a response to John Howard's political problems: he had to hold an election late in 2001 and was looking weak in the polls. One theory is that he adopted a tough position on refugees in order to gain a few votes from the supporters of Pauline Hanson.

Australian surveillance aircraft had sighted a boat, the *Palapa*, on its way from Indonesia to Christmas Island. It was carrying people seeking asylum. (Predominantly they were Hazara people from Afghanistan, fleeing the Taliban. Some things haven't changed in twenty years.)

The surveillance aircraft noticed that the *Palapa* was in trouble, about 140 kilometres north of Christmas Island. Australia radioed the MV *Tampa*, a Norwegian container ship which was in the area, and asked it to rescue the people on the *Palapa*. The *Tampa* soon found the floundering refugee vessel. *Tampa*'s captain, Arne Rinnan, thought the *Palapa* might be carrying about eighty people. He was astonished when more than 340 people climbed up a rope ladder from the *Palapa* onto the steel deck of *Tampa*.

Even though *Tampa* had rescued the people from the *Palapa* at the request of the Australian government, the government then ordered *Tampa* not to enter Australian territorial waters off Christmas Island – the closest land. When the *Tampa* disobeyed this order, SAS troops boarded the Norwegian vessel and took control of the bridge at gunpoint. That resulted in a stand-off, while the rescued refugees baked on the steel deck of the ship in tropical sun.

Litigation ensued. The trial judgement was in favour of the people rescued. It was handed down in Melbourne at 2.15 pm on 11 September 2001: just hours before the terror attacks on America began. Suddenly, the Australian government began calling refugees who arrived in Australia by boat 'illegals', even though their entry into Australia is not a criminal offence. The trial judgement was overturned shortly after, by a two-to-one majority in the full Federal Court.

Later, when Scott Morrison was immigration minister, the entire exercise (punishing 'boat people', sending them offshore, vilifying them) came to be called 'border protection'. The idea of locking up 'illegals' to protect ourselves sounds smart: until you realise that they have not committed an offence by coming here (so they're not 'illegal') and that it does not protect us to mistreat them. In short, the policy is based on two huge political lies.

The *Tampa* affair is a stain on Australia's reputation. Few other events have been as pivotal in the history of refugee and asylum policy in Australia, or so damaging to the fair treatment of people seeking safety. The Howard government manipulated the debate so it became divisive and polarising: 'us versus them', 'plane versus boat arrivals', 'refugees versus people seeking asylum'. The legacy of *Tampa* has been devastating for people seeking protection in Australia. Instead of offering safety, we punish people. Gone were compassion, fairness and decency, replaced with misinformation, dog-whistling and fear. The idea of the need for 'fortress Australia' – that our borders and community needed to be protected against boat people, labelled 'illegals' – took hold.

Seeking asylum is not a crime. Australia does not need to be 'protected' from people seeking asylum. Most of our federal politicians must either not know these facts, or be liars.

Calling people 'illegal' is politically clever. What do we do with criminals? We lock them up. Locking up 'illegals' sounds sensible. But when you learn that there are people in detention who have been there for ten years or more, without charge or trial or conviction, most people are horrified. The notion of treating people seeking asylum as if they were serious, convicted criminals begins to look very sinister.

Why does Australia detain people seeking asylum?

Australia is the only country in the world which has a policy of mandatory detention and offshore processing, although there is now a threat that other countries will follow our example. Mandatory detention was introduced in Australia in 1992 when the *Migration Act* was amended so as to identify a group of people who were 'non-citizens *without a visa*'. This was in response to an increase in boat arrivals (primarily from Cambodia). It is interesting to notice Article 14.1 of the Universal Declaration of Human Rights (adopted 10 December 1948), which says:

> Everyone has the right to seek and to enjoy in other countries asylum from persecution.

However, since then, Australia's detention regime has been extended and expanded. It has become arbitrary and long-term. Currently, the average time people spend in detention – 688 days – is the longest it's ever been. And more than 100 people have been detained for more than five years. Even alternative places of detention, such as hotels, supposedly used as a 'stop gap', are now being used to imprison people for longer than two years.

Anyone who arrives in Australia without a valid visa is detained in an immigration centre within Australia, including Christmas Island, or in an offshore detention centre on Nauru or Manus Island.

There are no time limits, either in policy or law, for how long a person, including a child, can be kept in immigration detention either onshore or offshore.

Numerous reports and inquiries have documented the harmful effects of detention. Despite this, mandatory detention and offshore processing remain a central part of both major political parties' policies in Australia.

Detention in Australia is used as punishment and to deter people from seeking asylum here. There is no reason to detain people. However, in circumstances where the government deems it 'necessary' for health or security reasons, detention should be for a maximum of 30 days for adults and 72 hours for children. Rather than recognise that people seeking asylum are fleeing persecution and fear for their lives, the current policy in Australia punishes people for seeking safety, especially those who arrive by sea.

How do Australia's current policies affect people while they wait for their refugee determination?

Rather than being welcomed, people seeking safety in Australia face punitive and discriminatory conditions while they wait for their refugee determination. For many people, even once they reach Australian shores, their search for safety is far from over. Many are locked up in mandatory detention. Those who are allowed to live in the Australian community are often not permitted to work and are not eligible for government support.

People in detention are denied their freedom. They have no idea how long they will be detained, or under what conditions. Use of force is common, as is being moved suddenly, late at night or early in the morning, to another detention facility. Once someone is in detention in Australia, they are out of sight – in the hope that they will also be out of mind.

For those living in the community while their protection claims are processed, their access to government support and opportunities available to them (work, study) depends on when and how they arrived in Australia and at what stage they are in the refugee determination process. Charities like the ASRC exist because the current policies do not enable people seeking asylum to live independently in the community or access a safety net if they need.

Even for many people who are found to be refugees, their protection is only temporary – with limits on access to support or safety nets like income support and Medicare.

One of the hardest aspects of Australia's temporary protection policy is that it doesn't allow family reunion. Temporary Protection Visas prohibit people from travelling outside of Australia or even applying for family reunion, and they have to apply for special exemption to leave the country if they want to see their spouse or children, who may still be living overseas.

Australia's treatment of people who come here looking for a safe place to live is, in a word, shocking. Our policies are bad, our application of the (very harsh) law is cruel. So politicians call people 'illegals' and the entire exercise 'border protection', and the public rest comfortably on the notion that we lock up criminals, to keep ourselves safe.

People seeking asylum not only speak different languages but come from radically different cultures to ours. That makes life very difficult for them here. We Australians think this is the best country on Earth, so we assume that is why people choose to come here. Most Australians have no understanding of the horrors people are seeking to escape by coming here.

The irony is that our political leaders are willing to mistreat people dreadfully if they have the nerve to come here seeking safety.

With over 90 per cent of Temporary Protection Visa holders between 1999 to 2008 being granted permanent protection, it is obvious that refugees need permanent protection, not temporary protection, to get on with their new lives. Temporary Protection Visas were reintroduced in 2014.

Temporary Protection Visas only last three to five years (depending on the type of temporary protection granted, a TPV or SHEV). If we want to take advantage of the skills brought here by refugees, they should be offered permanent protection. They are able to return to their country of origin whenever they want, if it is safe to do so: a visa entitles a person to live here. It is not a jail sentence.

It seems that the government has forgotten that the P in TPV stands for *protection*. And perhaps they have overlooked the fact that people coming here for protection do not come here on a whim: they come here to escape real danger.

What impact will the climate crisis have?

As the effects of climate change kick in, more and more people will seek a place where they can live safely. Many people will find it increasingly hard, or impossible, to make a living on land that is becoming drier or is repeatedly flooded. They are likely to look for other places on Earth where they can live safely. That's how human beings behave.

But fleeing climate change does not make you a refugee.

Because a 'refugee' is defined as a person who has crossed an international border 'owing to well-founded fear of being persecuted for reasons of race, religion, nationality, membership of a particular social group or political opinion', this definition does not typically extend to those who are displaced due to the impacts of climate change.

As the UNHCR notes, 'climate change affects people inside their own countries, and typically creates internal displacement before it reaches a level where it displaces people across borders. However, there may be situations where the refugee criteria of the 1951 Convention or the broader refugee criteria of regional refugee law frameworks could apply. People may have a valid claim for refugee status, for example, where the adverse effects of climate change interact with armed conflict and violence'.

So, while people forced to flee due to the climate crisis may not technically be refugees by the standard definition, we have an international obligation to respond adequately to the movement of people. Australia cannot afford to ignore the fact that in our own region internal and cross-border displacement within and from the Pacific Islands is likely to increase as disasters intensify and become more frequent, exacerbated by the impacts of climate change.

While Australia cannot stop the forced movement of people, we can implement policy changes now to reduce the scale and impact. We have a moral obligation to act proactively to mitigate human suffering caused by the climate crisis.

What's the solution?

Australia is an outlier in the way we treat refugees and people seeking asylum. We've changed laws to ensure our system is based on punishment and deterrence, rather than safety and protection, as it should be. Over the past decades, we have dehumanised people seeking asylum – starting with calling them 'illegal' (a lie) and continuing by accusing them of throwing their children overboard (another lie). Since 2001, a centrepiece of refugee and asylum policy has been to move away from our human rights obligations and base the debate on fear and misinformation. Legislation has been passed using manipulation and bullying tactics to secure votes for unnecessary and cruel policies.

In 2013 we even went so far as to pass a law that meant the entire Australian mainland was excised from the migration zone in a bid to deter the arrival of people seeking asylum. It sounds crazy but it's true – we removed Australia from its own migration zone. These are the lengths we have gone to in order to stop people seeking asylum in Australia. Scott Morrison has, in his office, a small model of a boat, with a sign saying 'I stopped these'. What a sad boast.

There is a devastating cartoon of an Aboriginal man standing at Sydney Cove on 26 January 1788. He is looking down at the First Fleet, lying at anchor in Sydney Harbour. He has a can of British Paints in one hand and has scrawled: 'Stop the Boats'. The irony could not be greater: his people had lived on this continent for over 40,000 years, and the First Fleet arrived here less than 240 years ago. British settlers treated Aboriginal people with the same inhumanity we see today in the treatment of people who come here seeking asylum.

The result of the 2013 change to the migration zone was that anyone seeking asylum by boat after 2013 wasn't technically seeking asylum in Australia (since legally the mainland wasn't part of the migration zone), meaning we could send them offshore to be processed. And that became compulsory in 2013.

Extending compassion, safety and protection is what's needed. The solution is quite simple, as we've done it before.

Between 1948 and 1992, Australia successfully and peacefully resettled 452,000 refugees. At this time, people seeking asylum were processed in the community and there was no policy of mandatory detention.

Most notably, after the Vietnam War, Prime Minister Malcolm Fraser introduced Australia's first refugee policy in 1977. The policy is the complete opposite of our refugee and asylum policy today. Between 1975 and 1982, Australia welcomed about 200,000 immigrants from Asian countries, including nearly 56,000 from Vietnam alone. As well, more than 2,000 Vietnamese people who arrived by boat without documentation were granted entry under policies initiated by the Fraser government.

This all happened without the fear, misinformation and political point-scoring that is the norm today. Asylum policy was based on compassion, not politics. We can and must return to asylum policy that is grounded in fairness and safety.

What needs to change?

Sometimes the best ideas are also the simplest. Treating refugees and people seeking asylum humanely and fairly would ensure they get the protection and safety they need and deserve. Our current policies come at huge personal cost and are intentionally and unnecessarily cruel.

Unfortunately, the way seeking asylum and refugees in Australia has been framed politically means they are seen as a threat – as 'us versus them'. Asylum and refugee policy has become entwined in conversations about border control and national security. This has had tragic consequences, resulting in loss of life, and harm to tens of thousands of people. The conversation is skewed. We really don't need to feel so threatened by the fact that people come here seeking protection from persecution of a sort we can barely imagine.

We can treat people seeking asylum with compassion, humanity and fairness and have secure borders. Other countries do this. It shouldn't be controversial.

It's up to us as a fair, democratic and caring society to see through all the politicking and make sure that people seeking asylum are not discriminated against. That they are offered a safety net while their protection claims are processed efficiently and effectively – and once found to be refugees are offered permanent protection in our country.

Part Two

Our Stories

Betelhem

I was on the boat for six days. I was the only Ethiopian, so I couldn't communicate with anyone. It was very scary and I was young – I turned twenty-one on the boat. We ran out of food and, on the fifth day, petrol. I didn't think we would survive. There was a big storm and the boat started to leak. On the sixth day, Australian Border Force found us and took us to Darwin.

After five days, guards came in the middle of the night and asked, 'Do you want to go to Nauru?' I didn't know what they meant. They told me there were education facilities there, good medical treatment and fair processes. I trusted them so I agreed to go.

Ten of us, all women, were taken to Nauru. When we arrived, we saw tents and lots of children and families crying. I was confused. Because I was the only Ethiopian, I couldn't understand what anyone was saying. For ten months we didn't have phones, television or radio, so there was no way to find out where I was. We were the first people transferred to Nauru and the detention centre was still being built. When we did get a phone, we were only allowed to use it once a month for fifteen minutes. If your family didn't answer, that was your chance gone.

Nauru was so hot. I'd never experienced heat like that before. For the first month, I vomited every time I ate. We were allowed one two-minute shower a day and we had to line up in the sun for it. The guards took our IDs while we showered. I didn't have any spare clothes, so I sewed new ones out of a sheet. I can't describe how bad the situation was. It was punishment, torture. The Australian government used our bodies as a human fence to stop the boats. Some of us died. We lost our friends, our time, our minds.

I lived on Nauru for fifteen months. I tried to survive by reading the Bible (I'm Ethiopian Orthodox) and studying English. I asked the guards to teach me two English words a day. If I had spoken English when they told me about Nauru, I would have refused to go.

My mental health suffered, and I was transferred to Brisbane for medical treatment. I thought this would help me feel better, but they locked me up again. Brisbane detention was the hardest experience of my life. Everyone there was from Nauru and they were always crying. When people shouted, self-harmed or were seized by guards, it made me even more stressed.

In 2016, a friend of mine was taken from our room in the middle of the night and transferred to Nauru. She set herself on fire and died. I saw what had happened to her on the news. We had slept next to one another in the same room for a year. I was devastated. It was Easter, so I called my family. My mother told me my grandma had passed away. My friend and now my grandmother. I had never felt so alone.

That's when I gave up. I went on a hunger strike and lost 5 kilograms in two weeks. After this, security guards watched me twenty-four hours a day. Even when I showered, I couldn't close the door. Every thirty minutes the guards wrote a report about what I was doing. I was in and out of hospital for a year.

After four years in detention I was told, 'You are free to go today.' I was shocked. Where would I go? I had no family.

I was given a place to stay for five months, but I wasn't used to being a free person anymore. I had forgotten how to use the phone, the TV, the oven. Everything. It was like being born again.

I was traumatised by what I had seen in detention, but I was strong. I studied for certificates in aged care, disability services and childcare. I wasn't allowed to study on my visa, but I traded cigarettes with people in exchange for them enrolling in Open College for me. In total, I completed more than ten certificates.

After five months they told me I had twenty-one days to find a place to live and a job. Until then I had not been allowed to work. I didn't know how to write a résumé and I didn't have a driver's licence.

Luckily there was a demonstration outside the immigration office on the day I signed my release papers. People were protesting against the bridging visa not allowing us to work or study. One of the protestors smiled at me and offered me a room. 'Don't worry,' she said, 'You can stay with me.' I was so surprised by this kindness from a total stranger. I stayed with her for a month while I found a place of my own.

Most of my friends are still in detention. I never want what happened to my friend in Brisbane to happen to anyone else. The ASRC provided me with four months of advocacy training. It wasn't easy. At first, every time they spoke about our experience in detention, I would cry, but the training made me strong and confident. Now I speak at rallies. When I do this, my mind becomes more peaceful. I have the microphone now and I am helping others.

I moved to Melbourne in 2019. It feels like home here. When I got a job with Metro as a ticket inspector, I was so happy. In detention they used to call me by my boat ID, 'TAS 16', but now my nametag says 'Betelhem'. I have my identity back.

Although I'm still not allowed to study on my bridging visa, I'm trying to study nursing this year. I don't believe you can lock up someone's brain.

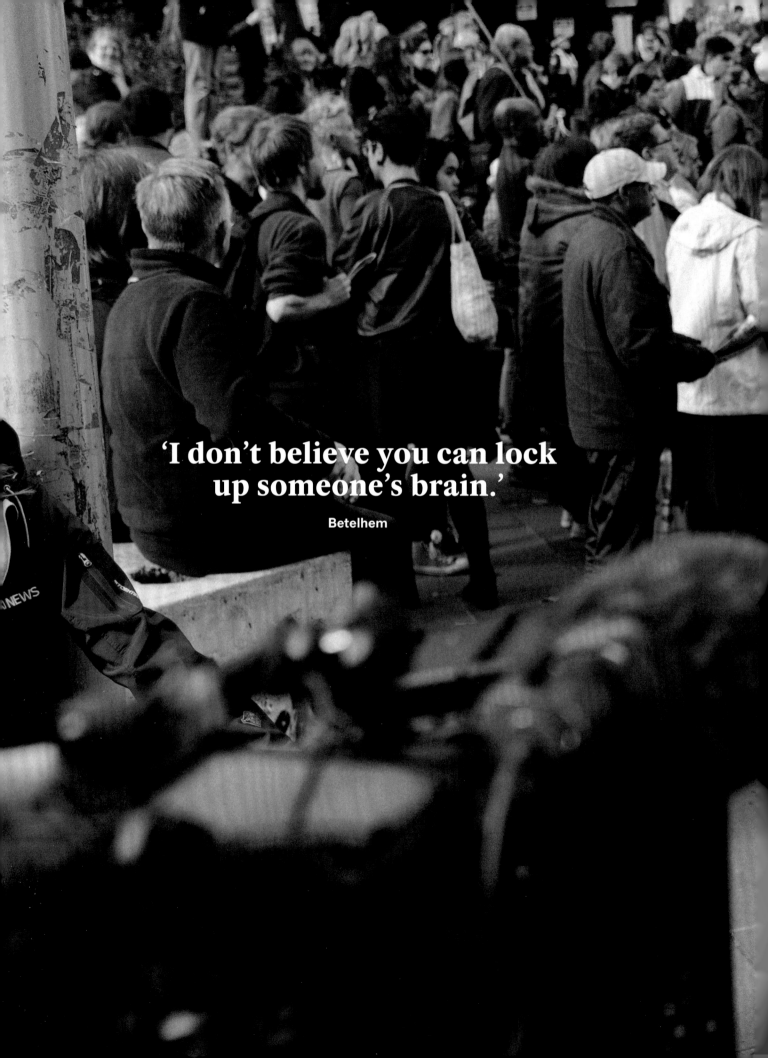

'I don't believe you can lock
up someone's brain.'

Betelhem

Ghofran

I loved primary school and as a child I dreamed of becoming a doctor. Inside the cover of our schoolbooks there was a picture of the president, Saddam Hussein. Under him, we were not able to safely speak our opinions and our freedom was restricted. One day I was drumming on his face with my pencil, thinking of all the things Saddam's government did that my father objected to. I tapped until I made holes in his eyes. If someone had seen this, it would have been very dangerous for my family: we could have been executed. I hid the book for an entire year inside our house. I didn't tell anyone, not even my mum. I was just nine years old, holding all this fear inside me.

When I was in Grade Six, my family fled Iraq and I missed a year of school. I spent six years in a Saudi Arabian refugee camp in the desert. Over 30,000 people lived there, in tents with no fridges or air conditioning. To cool down we would dip a bit of fabric in water and cover ourselves with it. But after five minutes it was dry again. There were no showers and long queues for the toilets.

One day the camp opened a school in a tiny caravan – I was so happy. When the teacher asked me what year I was in, I said I was in Year Seven because I didn't want to repeat a year. I had already lost so much time.

In 1999, when I was twenty years old, I came to Australia with my husband and eight-month-old son. We moved to Cobram, a country town in Victoria. We were one of the first Muslim families the locals had seen. And they were the first Australians we had seen. The first two years were the hardest. I had to get used to a new culture and language, and I was far away from my relatives. In the beginning, I was even too scared to go outside.

After living in Cobram for some years, I started to feel more settled, but that feeling soon turned to restlessness. I thought: *why don't I try to achieve my dream of becoming a doctor?* I'd always had this passion. When I told people I was leaving to become a doctor, no one believed I could do it. They said, 'It's too difficult,' or 'You have two kids, you have responsibilities.' I am grateful for their words of discouragement because they filled me with determination to prove them wrong.

When I moved to Melbourne in 2006 to study for my VCE, I had minimal literacy in English and I hadn't been to school for twelve years.

I pushed myself hard. I didn't have any support; I didn't even have the internet. For Chemistry, Maths and Biology, I had to translate

'Doctors might be able to cure your body, but teachers can cure your soul.'

Ghofran

every single word of the textbooks. I worked twelve hours a day, every day, and had two kids to look after as well. It was crazy. I completed my VCE with a score below 50, but I was really happy and proud of myself.

Because of my low score, no university wanted me. They couldn't see how far I had come. Fortunately, I was accepted into Victoria University's foundation studies course, which offers a pathway for disadvantaged students to improve their English skills and go on to medicine and other degrees. I completed the course and finished top of my class of about 150 students.

There were struggles of course: once I was told I'd failed my assignments because my English was poor. I had never failed in my life and I cried like a baby. I spent a week redoing all my assignments and resubmitted them. Later I received an email saying, 'Congratulations, you got a high distinction.' I still have this email today.

To say thank you to the university, I volunteered my time teaching other students in the foundation studies course. People kept saying that I was a good teacher, so I started thinking that helping other students to achieve their dreams might be even more rewarding than achieving my own. Doctors might be able to cure your body, but teachers can cure your soul.

After completing a Bachelor of Science (honours) with high distinction and receiving a Dean's Scholar award, I completed my PhD in the microencapsulation of natural antimicrobial agents.

Now I work as a lecturer, training biomedical students on their way to becoming doctors.

Victoria University opened the door for disadvantaged students. But opening the door is not enough: you need to recognise people's abilities in order to maximise their potential. I was lost in the crowd when I was doing my degree. I want to change that for other students, so now I sit on the University Council board. Disadvantaged students are more capable and passionate than those who haven't ever struggled. And you never know who you're talking to. If you support someone, they might be able to become a teacher, a social worker – or even the prime minister. Australia has welcomed many people seeking asylum who are now proud to belong here.

I have so often been the only Muslim woman in a room, but it no longer worries me. I know I am capable. I want to bring people together. You've read my story: having some doors opened for me enabled me to achieve my dreams. But I want you to know that my story could be someone else's story if they are welcomed into this country and given opportunities and their potential is recognised.

If you are a young person seeking asylum reading this, I hope that you know your dreams are possible. Believe in yourself and your ability to achieve your dreams.

I am proud to be Australian.

I am proud to wear a hijab.

I am proud of what I have achieved – for myself, my children and my community.

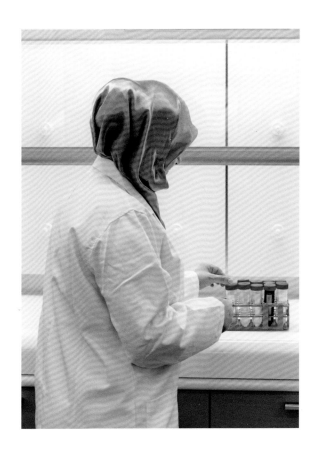

Hamed

I am a boat person. I like to say that to people. It is crazy to risk your life on a fishing boat, but I thought, 'If I'm going to die it's better to die in the ocean from a shark than at the hands of the Iranian government.'

My mother taught me to cook when I was fourteen. I have many happy memories of watching her prepare meals for our family. Once I was old enough, I asked Mum to let me cook too. It made me happy to see my family eating my food.

When I was eighteen, I moved into a share house with friends. I quit my job as a plumber and made a deal with my housemates: if I cooked for them, they would cover my rent. I didn't know how to cook many dishes to start with – only simple things like omelettes, spaghetti and rice. So I would call Mum and ask for advice. She was never in a rush and would patiently guide me through the dishes over the phone. Soon my friends were saying, 'Wow, your food is better than our mothers'.' After training and working as a chef in Tehran, I opened my own restaurant with two of my friends, it was a shisha shop, and a very successful business.

Unfortunately, I had to leave all this behind because of my religious beliefs. I was an atheist and it wasn't safe for me to stay; my life was in danger.

In Iran, if your parents are Muslim then you are a Muslim, it's even on your National ID certificate and you can't change that. If you do, then by law the government can execute you.

I only had one week to leave the country or I would be arrested. Everything happened so quickly. I found someone in the Tehran Grand Bazaar who could help me escape. I was trying to go somewhere nearby, like Turkey, Azerbaijan or Armenia. I never thought of coming to Australia, but that was the only option. I left everything behind. I didn't even say goodbye to my family or friends. If I communicated with them, they could also be arrested.

The fishing boat was small, there were 113 people on board but it only had capacity for sixty. We spent thirty-eight hours crammed tightly together – it was like dancing with death.

When I arrived in Melbourne, I handed out my résumé to over fifty restaurants and cafes all over the city, but nobody wanted me. They asked for Australian qualifications and references. Some said my English was not good enough. Only one person offered me a job, washing dishes for $8 dollar per hour. It would have been easy to give up, but I didn't.

I was lucky to find the Asylum Seeker Resource Centre. I joined the English classes and volunteered in the kitchen. I cooked Iranian dishes and discovered that many Australians hadn't tried Persian food. The feedback was always positive, and people kept asking if I had a restaurant. It was my dream to open my own cafe, and in 2019 I launched SalamaTea, a social enterprise that employs refugees and asylum seekers facing the same difficulties I faced when I first came to Australia.

SalamaTea is a small cafe but I employ as many people as I can. My goal is to train people and give them enough confidence to gain employment. It doesn't matter if they can't speak English or if they don't have qualifications or a reference; we take them on. Finding job opportunities is one of the most important things for people seeking asylum in Australia. So many people face the same difficulties I did when I tried to find work. The constant rejection can cause depression. People lose hope and don't feel like they are part of a community. I wish I had two or three SalamaTeas, so I could employ more people.

One of our most popular dishes is 'Dadami', which means 'from my father'. It is a very special recipe to me. When we were kids, whenever my father visited his sister in northern Iran, he would bring back a big tub of labne. We loved eating it, but we would get sick of it after a while. So Dad created this dip as a way of using up the leftovers. I remember Mum used to make a bread roll with Dadami in it for my school lunches. Now when I eat Dadami it brings back a lot of memories. It's more than just food. It's my culture.

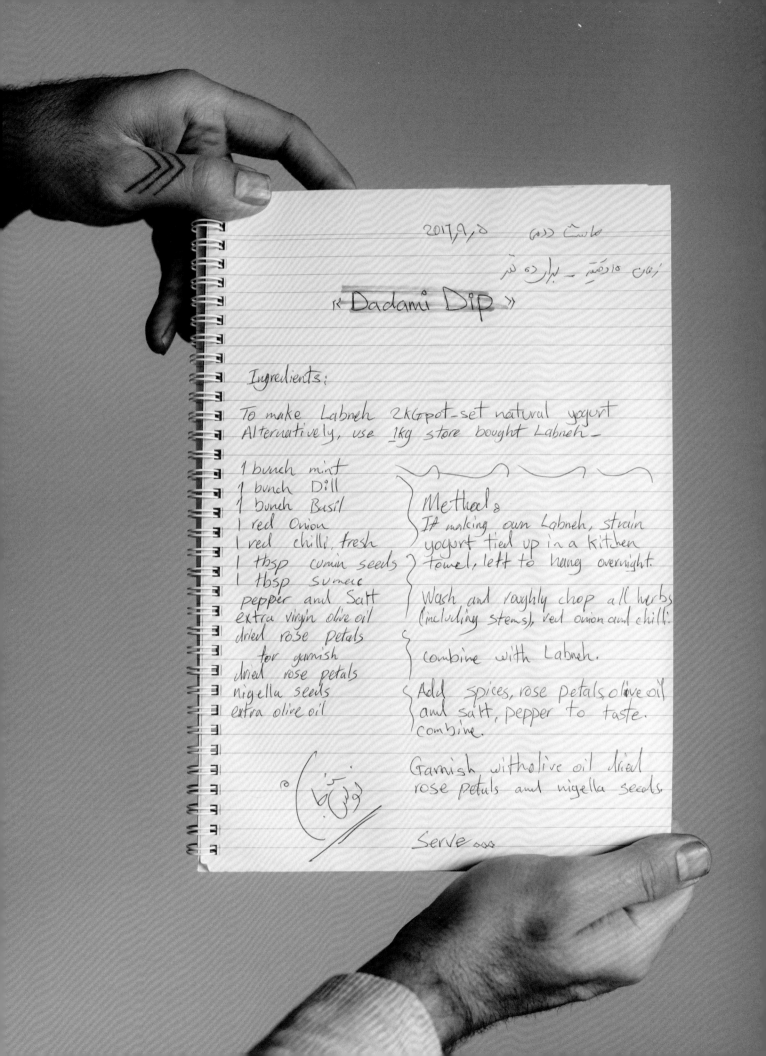

2017/9/5   مطبخ (٥٥)

نوعي ١٥دقيقة - لبراي ٦ نفر

« Dadami Dip »

Ingredients:

To make Labneh 2KG pot-set natural yogurt
Alternatively, use 1kg store bought Labneh.

1 bunch mint
1 bunch Dill
1 bunch Basil
1 red Onion   Method:
1 red chilli, fresh   If making own Labneh, strain
1 tbsp cumin seeds   yogurt tied up in a kitchen
1 tbsp sumac   towel, left to hang overnight.
pepper and Salt
extra virgin olive oil   Wash and roughly chop all herbs
dried rose Petals   (including stems), red onion and chilli.
   for garnish
dried rose petals   combine with Labneh.
nigella seeds   Add spices, rose petals, olive oil
extra olive oil   and salt, pepper to taste.
                        combine.

يمكن ٥   Garnish with olive oil, dried
                        rose petals and nigella seeds

                        Serve...

Kamal

I was twelve years old when I came to Australia. In the beginning, it was so exciting. My initial thought was: *this is literally paradise*. I'd never seen a beach in my life. There was food everywhere. It was really unbelievable. But pretty quickly, the paradise faded. I didn't speak any English and I didn't understand the culture, and that made it very hard to settle in my community.

I didn't understand why I was finding life here so difficult, and I felt hurt and confused. Later on, I realised okay, this is about racism. School was good, but as soon as we stepped out the door or onto a tram, or went to the local basketball court, people were not welcoming. They gave us a look that made us feel very uncomfortable. Kids would yell at us things like 'Go back to where you came from'. They'd start fights. There was so much intimidation, even in our own neighbourhood.

Racism is hard enough to deal with as an adult, but when you're twelve and you're trying to find connection, friends, belonging, it's even worse. I was raised to be tough, because we didn't have a lot. I used to walk 2 or 3 kilometres just to collect water. I was born in Ethiopia but I'm of Eritrean background. Back home, my dad had a good business and we had what we needed to survive – until the war began in 1998. One night my dad and two older brothers were taken away and we didn't see them

again for fifteen years. So even though the racism was terrible here in Australia, I didn't go home and tell my family. I kept it all inside.

Eventually, I became close friends with a neighbour who was half Somalian, half Australian. One day, we were playing soccer and he saw my skills and was like, 'What the hell is that?!' He took me to a local soccer club the following weekend. They gave me a shirt and put me in boots ten times bigger than my size. I remember that moment so well. I was way more advanced than all the other kids. I took the ball from the goalkeeper and dribbled all the way, scored, and did it again and again. I had no idea about positions. I'd never played in formations before. I didn't pass to the other players. Nothing. Just dribble, dribble, score.

Everything happened very quickly from there. After struggling to fit in, it was an unbelievable feeling to start playing for Port Melbourne. The team became my family: even though I still experienced racism outside, in the club I knew I was appreciated. It was not about the colour of my skin. They appreciated something that I had – my soccer talent – and for me at that time, that was good enough.

I got selected to play for Victoria thanks to one man – my mentor, Fred Dimitriou. If it wasn't for him, I would never have achieved anything. My dad

wasn't there, so Fred took me to every trial. He had his own kids and family, but he still drove me two, three hours to trials, fed me, took me home, told me I was going to play for Australia one day. He made me believe.

I got a scholarship to the Victorian Institute of Sport, and from there I was selected to play for the Australia Under-17 team. I had only been in this country for three or four years, and I didn't have a birth certificate. To prove my age, I had to do an MRI test where they look at a bone in your wrist. My first trip was to Japan, and it was an unbelievable experience.

I played for Australia for another two years, and the coach I had then was brilliant. He understood that I came from a different culture so when I was late to a meeting or didn't wear the uniform, I wasn't being disrespectful. It's just that I was brought up differently. He understood that when I was on the pitch I gave my best and I loved soccer just as much as anybody else. I never had a coach like him again.

Most coaches want you to be exactly the same as other players. They don't get to know you or understand your culture, so they punish you and then you lose confidence. I learnt that the hard way. The truth is, not everyone is the same. If a player hasn't been in Australia for long, they're still adapting to the culture. They're obviously going to make mistakes. Give them time to develop, give them time to learn. Eventually I did learn, but it cost me my career. I was never given a second

chance and I don't want other young kids to go through that. Coaches can make or break their careers – they need to be more open-minded and get to know their players, rather than punishing them because they're different.

At the end of the day, it wasn't meant to be. And maybe God had a different plan for me. I started a community soccer program, One Ball, in 2018. The program is about inclusion, diversity and belonging. It's so beautiful to see kids from all cultures, religions and backgrounds coming together. We create an atmosphere where everyone feels they can enjoy the game, without worrying about lack of money or skills.

The name One Ball comes from my experience back home. We didn't have fresh water, basic nutrition, television or video games, but we had one ball and that meant the world to us. One round ball brought everyone together in our community. It was a powerful thing.

Our sessions are about more than just soccer skills. For instance when we teach how to head a football, we use that as a vehicle to help kids build courage and believe in themselves.

Already 400 kids have been involved in the program. My dream is to give thousands of kids access to sports, not just to improve their physical and mental wellbeing but also to feel that they belong and are welcome in this community. Because once kids feel that sense of security, they can discover the superpowers that lie within them.

Nadira

I came to Australia as a refugee in 2004. I didn't travel here for the promise of a 'good life', to get a beautiful house and car. I had a successful career managing hotels in Beijing, but after speaking out about the Chinese campaign against my people, the Uyghur, I had no choice but to flee. I came to Australia for freedom. Every single day I hope I will return to my homeland.

In 2014 I opened the Uyghur Language School in Victoria. There are many Uyghur people like me, living in Australia because of persecution in China. I believe one day we will return to East Turkestan (Xinjiang) and I want our children to speak to their grandparents in their mother tongue. Some people say, 'You're dreaming', but we need dreams to keep our hope alive – and it may come true one day. China has completely banned speaking Uyghur, so if we don't teach our children the language then by the third or fourth generation it will be lost. The school is 79 kilometres from where I live, easily a one-hour drive, but I go every Sunday. I never feel like it's a chore. I love the kids, they fill up my heart.

There are many Uyghur orphans living in Turkey. China has imprisoned thousands of Uyghur adults for travelling to Muslim countries, even just for holidays, or for sending their children to study abroad. Their parents just disappeared from the airport. In 2018 I founded Make My Home, a charity to raise money to support these orphaned children. The word 'orphan' is not quite right: we don't know where their parents are, whether they're alive, or if they'll ever return.

Many of the students despaired completely when their parents were jailed, they couldn't stop crying – mentally, they were lost. I don't know if many Australians could understand this feeling. They tell us, 'We don't know where our parents are, we're not allowed to call them, they don't have the internet and there's no access to any media.'

China calls the prisons 're-education camps' but they are concentration camps. There are millions of Uyghurs imprisoned. First they arrested religious leaders, then writers, educators and artists. Now it doesn't matter what you do – if you are Uyghur, you are jailed. Inside the camp Uyghurs are not allowed to talk to each other, or pray. Women are raped. Every day hundreds of people die in the camps. They are killing us, our culture and our religion. It is genocide.

I don't have my own family in Australia, so I like to spend time helping my community. Over the past ten years I've written and translated the stories of more than a hundred Uyghur people seeking asylum to help them gain refugee status. The youngest was sixteen, the oldest seventy. People want to stay here because it's safe. There is no safety being Uyghur in China.

Many Australians only know what the Chinese have done to us. When they hear 'Uyghur' they imagine people dying and starving. But Uyghurs have a rich culture and 8000 years of history. We are famous for our complex music. The most well-known form is the *muqam*, which has twelve symphonies; it takes over two hours to play just one part. Portraiture is especially important in Uyghur art, and in East Turkestan there is cave art dating back thousands of years. Through the language school I'm able to pass on our culture. For special events we dress the children in traditional clothing printed with *etles*, a particular type of pattern, and *doppas* – embroidered hats worn to show wealth, marital status and for celebrations. I want to show the world who we really are.

Australia has given me and other Uyghur people a lot, and I want to thank Australians. I am working to become a justice of the peace – I want to give back to Australian people.

Joseph

My family were forced to flee our homeland, the Democratic Republic of Congo (DRC), during the Second Congo War – a decade-long conflict that cost millions of lives and left countless families displaced.

We found ourselves in Nyarugusu, an enormous refugee camp in Tanzania.

So here we were, far from home and heading towards an unstable future but yet more stable than the one we had left behind. Messing around one day, my friend and I caused some minor damage to a fence around an official government site in the refugee camp. One of the guards caught us and threatened to take us to prison. Of course we were terrified and started crying. My mother came over and talked to the guard and he eventually let us go.

And then we were in Dzaleka Refugee Camp ready to start over, again. Malawi is known as the Warm Heart of Africa and many of my memories from the six years we lived there are warm. There was a feeling of community in Dzaleka: everyone was in the same situation and working to make the best of it. There was a shared understanding that we had been pushed from our countries due to circumstances beyond our control. It was in our best interests to focus on the bright side. We supported each other through thick and thin, whether it was sharing sugar or lending money to the people going through tougher times. Some families with entrepreneurial aspirations were able to realise their dreams and they became examples for other refugees to follow.

I had never attended school because back in the DRC my family could not afford the tuition fees. As a kid, I was happy to stay home and not have to stress about things like homework. I didn't realise I was missing out on something vital for my personal development. It is estimated that over three million children in the DRC do not have access to school. Imagine the difference it would make if we were able to put them all in classrooms. The transforming effect on the country would be immense.

When people ask me where I come from, I tell them I'm from DRC. Some people ask how I can speak fluent English. I tell them about the six years my family and I spent in Dzaleka Refugee Camp. It was there that I started my schooling. I was eight years old by then. School was free in Dzaleka. Looking back, we were extremely fortunate to live there.

The more I learnt, the more I started understanding the world. My thinking was not just confined within the four walls of the camp. Through school, I came to understand the different climates around the world and how they affect agriculture. I learnt to add, multiply, subtract and divide numbers, and I started understanding what characters in American movies and TV shows were talking about. My world was expanding.

In September 2006, through UNHCR, we emigrated to Norway. There the schools were bigger, the curriculum more advanced, and the classrooms equipped with all the necessities to stimulate our minds.

After high school and many years away from study, I took advantage of support offered by the Norwegian government to pursue higher education in Australia, on the Gold Coast. I graduated in 2019 with a bachelor's degree in international business.

Now I'm back at university studying architecture. Among other things, I hope one day to start a practice and build environmentally friendly and affordable homes in developing countries.

Many things had to happen in my family's favour for us to end up in Nyarugusu, Dzaleka and Norway unharmed – and then for me to end up in Australia. We would not be in our current situation without the help of other people along the way. It took a community to get us here.

My parents had to leave their home for an unknown future. As a child, I did not grasp how big a decision that must have been. Now, as an adult I'm starting to understand the magnitude of that sacrifice – what it must have felt like to abandon their own dreams and aspirations to pursue a different future for us. They are my heroes.

'It took a community to get us here.'

Joseph

Rafique

My football career began in a refugee camp in Bangladesh. My brothers made a ball out of plastic bags. When I saw them playing with it, I wanted to play too. Our 'field' was a barren, rocky area of the camp. It was muddy and rubbish-strewn but it was there I fell in love with the game.

I was born in Cox's Bazaar, one of the largest refugee camps in the world. My mum always told my siblings and I that we didn't belong here because we were kicked out of our own land because we are Rohingya. In the camp we didn't have the opportunity to get an education. When I was young and it was raining in Bangladesh, I thought it must be raining all over the world. Many children in the camp still believe that today. It is the worst place you could ever imagine living. The houses are all open, and when it rained the government would just give us a plastic tarp to live under. Everything got wet and we couldn't sleep. In winter it was very cold and there were no blankets to cover ourselves with. We had seven family members living in a shelter just a few metres squared. It smelt awful because there was rubbish everywhere. There was no waste removal service and there was an open toilet next to where we slept. There was no clean water. Life was miserable.

The only time I felt free was when I played football with my brothers and friends. Then I forgot about everything else. We played every morning and afternoon. Focusing on the game saved us.

In 2009 the UNHCR resettled 10,000 people from the camp. We were lucky to be picked from among 800,000 refugees – we were the last family accepted. I moved to Australia with my family in 2010. From that moment on, our lives changed.

On my second day in Australia my cousins, who arrived here before us, took my family to a soccer field and showed us a real football. I held the ball for what felt like an hour. I started crying because I had never imagined I would be able to play with a real ball on a grass field.

I was twelve when we arrived in Australia. Starting high school was tough. I didn't know anyone, and I couldn't speak English. A few Aussie kids bullied and teased me in the classroom. But on the soccer field I could escape the hurt feelings. I focused on playing football and other people would come and join me. Once I could speak more English, I started sharing my story – where I came from and how hard my family's life had been – with the Aussie kids. They empathised with me and we started building friendships.

When I was studying IT at TAFE, I started listening to the news and learning about politics. I realised that the Australian government has betrayed refugees. They detain people who have

not committed any crime, simply for seeking safety and shelter. For many people living in the community, they withhold work rights and access to government support – so it feels like they're still living in a refugee camp, with no certainty or resources. It makes me so angry. Thankfully the Australian government did provide my family with the chance to come here, but they could be doing so much more. There are so many people who deserve to be living in a safe place and Australia could easily provide for them. My sister, cousins and friends are still living in refugee camps. When I think about them, I feel anxious and depressed. I'm scared of the government and worry that one day they might send us back to where we came from, even though we have Australian citizenship.

I experience racism every day. It doesn't matter how long I've lived in Australia: people still view me as 'different'. Even when I'm driving and I stop in traffic sometimes people will swear at me and say things like, 'Why did you come here?' In my previous job I was told 'You don't belong here', or 'You don't deserve this job'. It brings you down when you're surrounded by racism like that.

Soccer has completely changed my life, and I'm determined to give other refugees the same opportunity to grow through sport. I help connect refugees who want to play a sport with relevant community groups. Sport is one of the few areas in refugees' lives where they can feel free. It helps people make friends and feel like they belong.

For the past seven years, I've been coaching and managing the Rohingya United Brisbane soccer team. We have grown to a community league of twenty-four registered clubs. We never thought we would end up in a professional league. Playing with fellow Rohingyas feels like being part of a brotherhood and helps ensure we don't lose our cultural identity. Everyone speaks Rohingya and we eat traditional food. When we first started the team, some of my friends wanted to be like Aussies because of the racism they had experienced. They thought if they adopted Australian culture – had a barbeque and learnt how to eat pizza – they wouldn't be treated like garbage anymore. But I said no, we need to continue our culture. We share our water if someone forgets to bring it and we share food, because back in the camp we shared everything. It doesn't matter if we don't know each other; if someone is hungry, we invite them to join us.

Even when we lose a game, we still feel like we won. Who knows? Maybe one day we will play with other refugees from around the world. If we're given the chance, we can do great things.

Prudence

I was born in Chad, central Africa, in a little village called Beballem on a hot, steamy day. At first, life was perfect. Mum owned a small business and dad was a politician, so I had everything I needed as a child.

But one morning in 1999, when I was four years old, police officers knocked on our door and asked for my father. Fearing they were going to hurt us because my father had spoken up about government corruption, my mother took me and my two-year-old brother to hide under the bed. My father bravely opened the door and we heard a loud gunshot. We held our breaths and lay there petrified and drenched in tears, fearing the worst. Eventually the police officers left, taking my father with them.

Fearing that we were no longer safe in Chad, my mother decided we must flee. In the middle of the night, without saying goodbye to anyone, we left. We walked for many kilometres to a refugee camp in Benin. But after the long journey, the camp was full, so we slept on cardboard boxes outside the UNHCR office. After two months we were accepted into the camp.

All we had was each other. One morning, a camp officer came asking for Mum. I was terrified they would take her too. But he had good news. There was a man looking for us – it was my father. He'd survived and had escaped jail. My family was reunited.

For many years we held out hope that we'd be resettled in a new country. After seven years we were finally accepted – to Australia.

We moved to Toowoomba, a regional town in Queensland, in May 2007. The only words of English I could speak were 'thank you'. I thought it meant 'hello', so I thanked everyone I met, thinking I was greeting them.

When I started school, I immediately felt misunderstood by my peers. They didn't know why I had come to Australia, and my skin colour, accent and hairstyle were unfamiliar to them. When I pulled out my lunch, they'd say 'eww, that's disgusting!' This was the start of my experience of racism in Australia. It made it really hard for me to make friends.

One day I got off the bus and was walking home and someone threw a bag of trash out the window at me and yelled 'go back to where you came from, you don't belong here'. That was a very scary moment for me.

But despite these challenges, growing up in Toowoomba was great in many ways. Although I experienced racism, I had enough of a support system to be a voice for those that were too scared to speak up for themselves. Towards the end of high school, I researched programs that educated young people in schools about refugees, migrants and racism. I was disappointed to discover that there

were no such programs in Queensland. I created E-raced to fill the gap.

E-raced is an organisation of young refugees and migrants who visit schools in regional and rural Australia and share their personal stories with staff and students. Storytellers share their stories to build understanding and acceptance and create a more diverse, accepting and welcoming Australia for everyone. They put a face to experiences Australian kids may have only heard about previously on television.

Interacting in person is so powerful. When someone is sitting face to face right in front of you, you get an opportunity to see them for who they really are. You hear them talk, see them smile, listen to their stories. And you realise this person is a human being just like yourself. It leaves you feeling more connected. This increased comprehension and empathy means that racist attitudes and viewpoints can be challenged and changed.

As Michelle Obama once said, 'It's hard to hate up close.' No one is born a racist. Racism is the result of learned attitudes and behaviours that go unchallenged, and a fear of the unknown. But it can be erased, one story at a time.

Refugees' stories are not heard often enough. People don't really understand the depths of what refugees go through. Their stories are ones of courage and determination. Whether you're a refugee or not, you can learn something from their experiences.

Racism affects kids' confidence. They develop low self-esteem and mental health issues. It leads to young people not wanting to go to school, to them being depressed, even to suicide. It happens every day, right under our noses, and we don't see it. Sometimes when kids misbehave or become criminals, it's because of these experiences. Early experiences of racism can affect them long-term.

If Australia wasn't racist, we wouldn't need to advocate against racism every day. The more you advocate, the more you get people sending you threatening messages. What do you call that if it's not racism?

Storytelling brings out a lot of revelations. Recently at a school in Melbourne, we got kids to come together and share their experiences of racism. The classroom teacher had no idea that her students were going through these things every day. We asked a student 'When did you last encounter such behaviour?' and he said, 'This morning at school.' The teacher bawled her eyes out because she hadn't known. The students having that safe space to share those stories opened her eyes – now she will be more aware and know to check in on these students and they'll know to look out for each other.

My dream is to be in a position where I can contribute all the skills that I have applied over the years, through my legal work, and through E-raced.

My dream is to make the subject of racism not so uncomfortable for people. I want people to feel safe to talk about it, it's okay to seek help and learn how to become an ally. We can't erase racism by ourselves. Only if we accept that there is an issue and all work together will things change.

Danijel

I was ten years old when I won my first wage theft case. It was my own wage.

My family were living in a refugee camp in Serbia, and I worked alongside my mother on a dairy farm. I had to work because humanitarian aid had ceased, due to sanctions placed on Serbia in the late 1990s. I helped with the milking by corralling cows into bays, wiping down udders and scraping dung into running sewers with a shovel. I was kicked, trampled and gored in the process.

On one occasion, the dairy owner refused to pay our wages for the entire month. He wanted to see if he could get away with it. He taunted us by pointing out that we were stateless refugees with no recourse to the law. 'Where will you go? Who will help people like you?' he sneered. All his workers were internally displaced refugees from the Croatian War of Independence. To add insult to injury, he named his cows after the women who milked them.

With the fall of communism in the 1990s, the owner had become a 'red bourgeoisie' – someone who made money out of the changing situation, while pretending to be a communist. As well as the dairy, he owned a local grocery store.

After our shift finished, my mother and I walked into his shop and filled our trolley equal to our combined unpaid wages for the month. We walked out without paying a cent. The shop clerks tried to stop us. My mother kicked at them with her gumboots caked with cow-dung. They backed down. We walked back to the refugee camp with our trolley full of food. He was never late with our wages again.

I share this story because when we talk about refugees, we run into the 'danger of the single story', as Nigerian writer Chimamanda Ngozie Adichie wrote. The danger in the case of refugees is that we are seen mainly through the lens of displacement. But refugees are seldom affected in only one way. We come with layered, often unseen, identities.

Take my mother, for example: she was a refugee, yes. But she was also an internally displaced person (IDP). A stateless and undocumented woman. A woman in a patriarchal setting working in labour-intensive male-dominated industries. A war widow. She was a Croatian woman who found herself across 'enemy' lines.

But you wouldn't know about any of these distinct and separate identities and human conditions if you only saw her through the narrow lens of a 'refugee'.

At least we had work. We heard that people across the border in Bosnia could not work because their capital was under siege. There, snipers in the mountains picked off people as they stood in line to collect water. To eat, you had to donate blood. For 300 millilitres of blood extracted from your body at the main hospital in Sarajevo, you received a can of Spam. Beef for blood, it was called.

Fast-forward fifteen years. It is 2016, I am sitting in a cafe outside the Fair Work Commission in Melbourne, Australia. I am now a lawyer. I have gone from milking cows in a war zone to representing blue-collar workers in Australian courts. I speak English fluently. With pomaded hair neatly parted,

a good-quality moisturiser and a tailored suit, no one can tell I was once a stateless refugee covered in cow-dung, stuck in back-to-back wars.

I have just finished representing an Australian worker who was unfairly dismissed from his job. We're grabbing a coffee after the hearing.

As we talk, he begins complaining about refugees. He says he has heard the Minister for Immigration say on the radio that 'they' are coming to take jobs from Australians. That 'they' will be a burden on the welfare system. That 'they' are illiterate and innumerate. That 'they' do not assimilate.

I feel an almost visceral urge to confront this man. To tell him about the realities of war. To explain to him that he is speaking to one of 'them'. That I am not a faceless threat but a human being with a name, made up of bone and blood. That I am not an anonymous exile trying to steal his job. That in fact I – a refugee – just got him his job back.

I want him to realise there are no neat categories of people, orderly queues, easy answers or simple facts. There is only us: sharing common humanity and a common destiny. I want him to see through the racist framing the minister wants him to swallow. This agenda deceives low-paid, Award-dependent white working-class people like him by stoking animus against people like me.

But instead, I choose silence. The words of Holocaust survivor Elie Wiesel sting in my ears: 'to forget would be not only dangerous but offensive; to forget the dead would be akin to killing them a second time.' I think of those who died in war and feel guilty for not speaking up. But it does not feel like a safe space for sharing.

Gaining this visa changed our lives. This is why I have faith in international law and the UN bodies and will continue my advocacy to make sure we respect international norms and customs. In 1954, Australia's signature brought into force the 1951 UN Convention relating to the Status of Refugees. We should be proud of that legacy, but instead our government is trying hard to extricate us from the very laws our signature brought to life. As the second UN Secretary-General Dag Hammarskjöld said, 'The United Nations was not created to take mankind to heaven, but to save humanity from hell.'

The woman in the red jumper is my mother. I took this photo inside the dairy farm the week she was advised by the United Nations that she won the refugee lottery: Woman at Risk Visa (Subclass 204). A visa for women and their dependents subject to persecution in their home country or registered as being 'of concern' to UNHCR and without the protection of a male relative.

I am moved every time I read the phrase 'of concern'. At a time when nobody cared about my mother, the UNHCR cared. This is one of the few photographs I have of her smiling and not wearing black. With news like that, how could you not smile?

Danijel Malbasa
Form Yugoslavia

In the years since, my mother has fought a Kafka-esque battle with the Serbian government to receive her pension. When she lodged a claim for her pension with the Serbian Department of Veterans Affairs, they said her husband fought for the Yugoslav People's Army (JNA), not the Serbian Army, and because Yugoslavia no longer existed neither did her pension. It was as if her husband never lived, never served in the army, never died in service to Slobodan Milošević's vision of a 'Greater Serbia'.

Aghast at this response, she organised a collective of other widowed refugee women in the same situation and filed legal proceedings against the government of the Republic of Serbia in the European Court of Human Rights in Strasbourg, France.

One day, she suddenly received $25,000 into her account. It is a fraction of what she is owed. She continues her fight. I stay out of it, finding the whole affair somewhat comical. But from a distance, I draw inspiration from her strength, tenacity and determination.

As well as working as a union lawyer, I 'pay it forward' by volunteering at Refugee Legal Inc., helping people seeking asylum apply for Temporary Protection Visas or Safe Haven Enterprise Visa.

In this photo I am moving the admission for a Somali refugee, Lucky Giire, to become a lawyer. She is the first Somali female lawyer admitted in Australia. I am wearing robes borrowed from Yasar Bakri, a Melbourne barrister whose parents are Palestinian refugees. Three generations of refugees, captured in one image.

Tenzin

The lingering memory of my father is the sound of his flute. I don't remember his face, only his long hair. The tunes from his bamboo flute and my mother humming while herding the flock of yaks and sheep in the mountains has had a lasting influence on my life as a musician.

From their remote refuge, my nomadic parents escaped into exile in the early 1970s when the Cultural Revolution raged across the Tibetan Plateau. Crossing the mighty Himalayas, they made their way to Nepal, where my father passed away. Misfortunes stacked up in my mother's life and she had to negotiate fast to a new way of life.

She soon realised that her children needed modern education. Therefore my younger brother and I were sent to the Tibetan Children's Village in North India. I was around four. We waited on a railway platform where this long thing that looked like a series of moving houses on wheels pulled in.

'Study hard and make sure you get a good position in a chair,' my mother advised me. As a former nomad and refugee, encountering the modern world for the first time, she thought that a good job was to 'sit on a chair in an office'.

We boarded the train and bid goodbye to my mother.

At the refugee school, I was given a date of birth, since I didn't know the real one. And so, for over a decade, I lived in this school, where I grew up with over

3000 other children – learning, playing, fighting and having fun. This was our substitute 'home' but one with wonderful experiences and lasting memories. In this warm and affable environment, we often forgot that we were separated from our parents. Most of the friends I meet these days, while touring around the world, are the ones I grew up with in the school. Denied the opportunity to go back home to Tibet – because it has been occupied by the Chinese Communist Party – we have scattered around the globe, finding new homes in strange countries.

As I was finishing high school in India, my mother passed away. Pain knotted in my chest. A part of me was gone forever. I tried not to falter and went on to study economics and geography at an Indian university. After graduation I got a job with the Tibetan Institute of Performing Arts, where I thought I might be able to study music. However, in a curious twist of fate, I was made a shopkeeper.

In the shop I spent more time playing the musical instruments than selling them. My earliest childhood memories returned and music came calling. Time was on my side and so was opportunity. I found my small world in this tiny shop. Around this time an Australian volunteer teaching English at the institute frequented the shop. Before long she became a friend and the rest is history. I immigrated to Australia with a suitcase and my instruments, as her partner. Music wasn't high on my list of things to do. But if I missed home, I could play music to assuage my heart, I thought. However, a chance opportunity to perform at the University of Queensland lit a beacon in my life.

I met Pat and Sim Symoms after the performance and they spoke about the Woodford Folk Festival, which they run. 'Do you want to come and do a concert there?' they asked. I was a greenhorn to music festivals, but I said yes. I am proud and honoured to say that I've never missed this incredible festival since.

Deeply rooted in my Tibetan heritage and especially my nomadic background, I started writing music and over the decades I've produced over a dozen albums. I've also had opportunities to collaborate with an extraordinary number of musicians from many different genres. They truly enriched me and my art.

To me, music is like sublime boundless clouds drifting across geographical boundaries, creating common ground for human beings. I've presented my music on various global platforms and also in the presence of the Dalai Lama. These were my proudest and humblest moments.

When Tibet lost its freedom and when thousands of Tibetans were forced into exile, everything was strange to us in foreign lands. Only the sky and the earth were familiar. Under the charismatic leadership of the Dalai Lama, we've withstood the trials of time and re-established what was destroyed in Tibet – our community, our language, our culture, our music and our spiritual practices.

People of my parents' generation were always ready to return home – they had their suitcases packed and shoes ready under their beds. After over sixty years since our country was occupied, most of them have passed away without ever realising their dream to see their homeland again. As an artist, I have hope and faith that we can fulfil this dream. I get up each morning with renewed strength – and hope to sing, play my dranyen and tell my story.

I must live. I must sing.

Rahila

I was born in Quetta, Pakistan. Our life there wasn't easy. It was normal for me to go to sleep hungry or not to be able to buy supplies for school. In the society I was born into, equal rights were not valued. Some people even considered girl children a sign of shame. But my mother always reminded my siblings and me that we should be thankful to God because there were people whose lives were harder than ours.

In 2013, when I was twelve years old, a bomb blast changed my life forever. I was at a friend's house when we heard a huge explosion. The windows shattered and we rushed outside to find that half the sky had turned black. People were crying and racing to find their loved ones. That day, my life turned as black as the smoke in the sky. The sound of the bomb kept coming back to me. More than a hundred people died in the blast. Four of them were students from my school. In those two seconds, my hopes and dreams died too. From then on, shooting and bomb blasts became everyday events in Quetta.

But my relationship with God was very strong and I told myself that God had a greater plan for me. I needed to give life another chance.

In 2014, my family and I were granted humanitarian visas to come to Australia. I was terrified, because we were leaving everything we knew behind, but I was also ready to start a new life.

'All I wanted was a life where I could fall asleep safely, go to school and be treated the same.'

Rahila

When I arrived in Brisbane, the first things I noticed were the heat, the blue sky and the smell: different and fresh. In Australia, I had many new experiences – sitting on a swing in a park, catching a bus, using a trolley for grocery shopping, and most importantly going to school and making Aussie friends. But my new life was bittersweet. Along with all the freedoms, I had to endure comments such as 'Go back to where you came from' or being called 'terrorist'. My biggest fear was not being accepted because I am Muslim and wear a hijab. However, I wanted to do something with my life, so I knew I had to step out of my comfort zone.

First, I had to learn how to love myself. Whenever I left the house, I told myself, 'Rahila, you are beautiful.' I started to go out in public more and got more involved at school. I won a local art competition and gave a speech on Human Rights Day. In 2017, I was commissioned to paint part of a Cultural Wall in Toowoomba. For my leadership, volunteering work and dedication to empowering women worldwide, I received an award from Zonta and a bursary from the National Council of Women of Queensland. In 2019, I won the ADF Long Tan Leadership and Teamwork Award. Through my public speaking and community work, I have been able to break down negative stereotypes and present a good example to future generations.

In 2020, I won the ABC Heywire storytelling competition and got to travel to Canberra, where I met other young inspiring storytellers from around Australia and visited Parliament House, my dream workplace.

Living in Australia, I feel like my hopes and dreams are achievable again. Now my dream is to enter parliament one day. I believe in equal human rights. No one deserves to be treated differently because of their religion, race, skin colour or gender identity.

My experiences have made me appreciate life. When I think of Pakistan, I remember how many people are still in need. Coming to Australia was a life-changing experience. I don't ever want to take it for granted.

It's human to expect life to be easy. We all have dreams and expect our lives to go to plan. When they don't, many people give up. But we all experience hardships, big or small, and these experiences make us stronger. It is okay to cry or be scared, but we should not give up.

I will never forget my home country, Afghanistan, but if I do something in the future, I will do it for Australia and its people, because they have gifted me a new life. As a future leader, I want to shut out my own voice now and listen to the voices of those who are not as fortunate as me.

Rahila

Batoor

I am a Hazara. The homeland of our people is Afghanistan. Like thousands of other Hazara kids, I was born in exile. The ongoing oppression of my people forced my parents to leave Afghanistan. This persecution dates back to the late 1800s and the rule of Abdur Rahman, who killed over 60 per cent of the Hazara population and built minarets with their heads.

Many Hazaras were sold into slavery; others fled the country for neighbouring Iran and Pakistan. My family fled to Pakistan and settled in Quetta, where I was born.

I got my first chance to go to Afghanistan after the September 11 attacks in the United States. I was just eighteen and got a job working as an interpreter for foreign journalists.

A few years later I started working as a documentary photographer, and in 2005 moved permanently to Afghanistan. One of the most important issues I covered was the Dancing Boys of Afghanistan – a tragic story about an appalling tradition. Young boys are made to dance for warlords and other powerful men. They are often abducted – or bought from parents living in poverty – and are put to work as sex slaves.

When this story was published in *The Washington Post*, I started receiving death threats. I was forced to flee Afghanistan as my parents had done years earlier.

I returned with my mother and siblings to Quetta. The situation there had changed dramatically. Once a peaceful haven, it had now become the most dangerous city in Pakistan. The Hazaras in Quetta are confined in two small areas. They are marginalised socially, financially and educationally. Around 1600 members of the Hazara community had been killed and 3000 injured, many of them permanently disabled. And the attacks would only get worse.

Australia is home to the fourth-largest population of Hazaras in the world. When it came time to flee Pakistan, Australia seemed the obvious choice. Financially, only one of my family members could leave. It was decided that I would go, in the hope that if I arrived at my destination safely I could work to get the rest of my family to join me later.

No one makes such a decision lightly. If I could have flown to Australia, it would have taken less than twenty-four hours. Instead, my journey was much longer, more complicated and far more dangerous. I travelled to Thailand by air and then by road and boat to Malaysia and into Indonesia. I paid people smugglers along the way and spent a lot of time hiding, in fear of being caught.

In Indonesia I joined a group of seven refugees in Bogor, a town outside Jakarta. All eight of us shared a bedroom. While I waited to find a smuggler for the boat trip, I documented the daily lives of these people.

These photographs were taken by Batoor, documenting his journey from Afghanistan to Australia.

On my first week in Bogor, three of my roommates – Jaffar, Nawroz and Shabbir – left on the perilous journey by sea. Two days later we got the news that a distressed boat had sunk en route to Christmas Island – only Jaffar survived. It made me wonder: am I doing the right thing? But I concluded I had no choice but to go on.

A few weeks later the call came from the people smuggler. Ninety-three of us boarded an old fishing boat that was already overloaded. Around eighty-nine of us were below deck – no one was allowed up on top. We had each paid US$6000.

The first night and day went smoothly but by the second night the weather had turned. Waves tossed the boat around and the timbers groaned. People below deck were praying, crying, vomiting. We lost all hope. We thought: *this is the end*. Water poured in faster than the pumps could push it out.

We went above deck and flashed our torches to attract the attention of passing boats. The captain told us our boat was not going to make it. We kept trying to get attention by waving life jackets and whistling. Eventually we made it to a small island, the boat crashing onto the rocks. We scrambled over submerged rocks to get to shore. I slipped into the sea and destroyed my camera but luckily the memory cards survived.

The island was covered in thick jungle. We split up into groups as we argued over what to do next. We were all scared and confused. After a night sleeping on the beach, we hailed a boat from a nearby resort and were quickly handed over to the Indonesian water police.

At Serang detention centre, an immigration officer strip-searched us and took away our mobiles, shoes and my $300 of cash. We carefully watched the guards' movements and at 4 am, as they sat around a fire, we saw an opportunity to escape: we removed two glass slats from a window and slipped through it. We climbed a tree next to an outer wall that was topped with shards of glass. We put our pillows over the glass, wrapped sheets around our forearms and climbed over the wall.

I had no future and nothing with me but my memory cards. A documentary about my life and journey was aired on SBS *Dateline*. After that, I decided to stay in Indonesia to process my refugee claim through UNHCR. Many of my friends came to know about my situation and they all tried to help me. I was afraid that I would end up in Indonesia for years, with no work rights, like other refugees – but I was lucky: my contacts helped expedite my case through UNHCR and I was resettled in Australia in May 2013.

Not every refugee is lucky like me and it is really difficult to live with your fate in limbo.

The issue of refugees in Australia is framed as a political issue rather than a humanitarian one.

The Australian government would have confiscated my camera and memory cards if my journey by sea had been successful. The world wouldn't have seen these images of a humanitarian disaster. The images I captured are my testimony of the crisis – which is only getting worse. I was one of the few lucky ones who got to safety quickly; many don't reach their destinations at all and end their lives as refugees.

Tom

I escaped from Vietnam on a boat and arrived as a refugee in Australia in 1979. At eleven years old, I was alone in a strange country without any of my family.

The boat that carried 150 of us was very small, about 15 metres long and 3 metres wide. We were packed together tightly, with only enough room to sit, hardly any room to move. A few days into our voyage, we were captured by a Thai fishing boat. The Thai fishermen-turned-pirates searched everyone and robbed us of all the valuables they could find. We were scared, hungry and weak. Hoping that they would allow us to continue on our way, we complied with their demands. Mercifully, they gave us some food and water and let us go.

We were only able to travel for one more day before we were attacked by another Thai fishing boat. Unlike the last boat, this group of seven pirates was very ruthless. Armed with knives, they forced most of us to get on their boat, where they had room to search us more thoroughly for our remaining valuables. The women and some men were herded into the fish-hold. As a child, I didn't understand how dire our situation was, but the hopelessness and despair in those around me was palpable. Looking back, I now realise that had those pirates been successful in their plans, all the men would have been killed and the women and children would have become victims of human trafficking.

The pirates began to ram our boat with theirs in an attempt to sink it. Faced with the choice between fighting for our lives or being killed, our men chose to fight and were able to overpower the Thai pirates and seize control of their boat. We lost three brave men that day, one of whom left behind two children even younger than me. Their mother was many kilometres away, still in Vietnam.

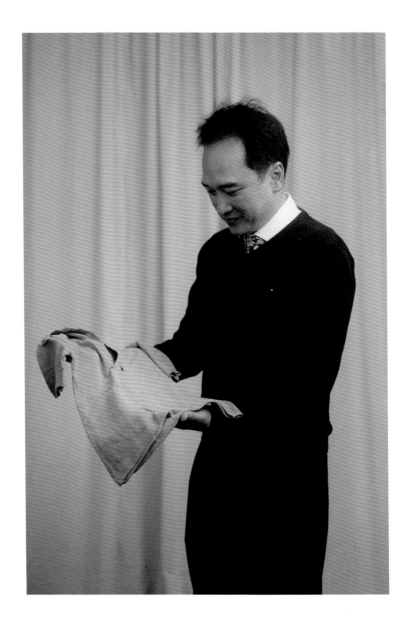

We continued towards our destination for another few hours before the engine broke down. We spent the next two weeks or more drifting in open water. There was enough water on the Thais' boat but the food supply dwindled until it ran out completely after a week. We began to accept that we were going to perish at sea.

Just as we were losing all hope, by some miracle an English oil tanker stumbled upon our boat. They welcomed us to their vessel, rescuing us, and brought us to Darwin. After being without food for so long, I was too weak to even stand by myself and needed to be lifted onto the tanker. I remember thinking that I was so lucky to survive.

I still have the t-shirt I wore on that boat to Australia. Looking at it now, I am reminded of how small I was when I went on that incredible journey.

Over forty years later, the ordeal still haunts me. But after my arrival in Darwin, I received so much support from the Australian people and the Australian government to help me settle into my new life.

At fifty-three, my life looks very different from the one I left behind. I'm married, blessed with four children and I run a pharmacy in Footscray. I love the diversity here. I meet people from all over the world and I work with many people seeking asylum through my work with the Asylum Seeker Resource Centre (ASRC). I am grateful to be able to work so closely with the ASRC. This amazing organisation helps those seeking asylum by covering the cost for people who are denied Medicare cards, ensuring they have access to life-saving medications.

I have always felt welcomed in Australia. Unfortunately, many people seeking asylum today, particularly those who have come here by boat, have not received the same warm welcome I had. Instead, many have been detained and often faced harsh living conditions affecting them physically and mentally while waiting – in many cases, for years – to be legally accepted as permanent residents.

We live in a great country. Here we are able to live safely without the fear of persecution, and have the freedom to speak our minds. These are some of the reasons why some refugees fleeing their countries choose to come to Australia.

I was lucky to have the opportunity to build a life here in Australia. But it shouldn't be a matter of luck. Everyone should have the right to seek protection. I hope that soon this will be a reality for all those who seek asylum.

Niro

There were a lot of NGOs working in Sri Lanka and the staff were mostly Western people, white people. We felt if we went to the white people's place, we would be safe. When I travelled to Australia, I thought I was going to the right place to live peacefully. I applied for asylum because I experienced such terrible conditions in my life back home and I wanted to start again in a new safe place.

But after I came to Australia in 2009, I was locked up in immigration camps for nearly six years. It was a horrible situation because we didn't have any choice. Everything was provided by Serco (management) or Immigration. It didn't matter if you stayed one day or one week or six years. There was no choice. This made us feel very stressed. Twenty-four hours a day, we were living in this small place with a security fence and cameras. Just like in a prison, the guards searched our rooms and sifted through our belongings during monthly inspections.

I was held because I received a negative security clearance from ASIO. They said I was a dangerous person, a danger to the Australian community. I had had only two short interviews before they gave me this negative security clearance. I don't believe the people who interviewed me could understand what my life was like in Sri Lanka or the situation there politically and economically through such short interviews. Most Sri Lankan Tamil people have fled persecution, leaving

everything behind to find a safe place to live. I was nearly twenty-nine years old when I came here. And after four, maybe six, hours these people decided my fate.

For the next few years, I received the same answer: you are not eligible to be granted a visa. The minister will not allow you to leave. And we are looking to resettle you in some other country. That made me worry: *what's going to happen to my future?* I lost a lot of my life in the immigration camp. Each day, just waking up, eating and sleeping. Just those three activities for six years. That's not a normal human life.

On Christmas Island, at Weipa in Queensland, and Port Augusta in South Australia there were people from several countries and Serco provided the meals. But after we moved to the Broadmeadows camp, I was with Sri Lankan people and we got the chance to cook our own food. We said, 'We've been locked up such a long time, we need to eat our traditional meals.'

After three years we started to eat our own rice and curry, a very spicy curry, and we said, 'Ah, we've missed it so much for all these years.'

Back home, I was not involved in cooking. My mum would cook everything. I had only sat next to her and watched what she was doing. But I joined the cooking team at Broadmeadows and learnt from my friends.

The taste, I knew. So, for example, if I was going to cook dhal curry, I knew that taste, but

I didn't know the structure or which order to use the ingredients in. That's what I needed to learn. My tongue could say, 'Ah, this is the taste', or 'There's something missing, this is wrong.' So, I followed my tongue and I improved.

After my release from immigration, I had the chance to be involved in a project called Tamil Feast. We would make our traditional meals and around eighty guests would come and have dinner with us. I learnt even more about cooking. After that, I realised I'd been cooking for more than ten years; that gave me the confidence to start a food stall.

I started cooking a Sri Lankan street food called *kothu roti*. It has three parts – chopped roti, vegetables and curry, mixed together on a hot plate. Every evening anywhere in Sri Lanka, you can hear this sound of people making *kothu roti – tuka tuka tuka tuka*. So, I called my business Tuka Tuka Kothuroti Man. It's getting popular and I work at a few markets now. It makes me very happy to make this dish. Melbourne people like food. When I make it at a market stall, a lot of people come and watch me. Some people have never tasted it before, but others have been to Sri Lanka or India and they know the sound: *tuka tuka*. They follow the sound.

I'm growing and still learning. If I grow a little more, I'm going to employ other people. That's my dream – to give an opportunity to someone else.

Gordon & Paul

Gordon: We have always played music. I play the thom (a wooden banjo-like instrument from the Upper Nile region) and my cousin Paul plays the drums with me. In Sudan we had a band of six or seven people. We toured all around Africa and even to Australia and the USA. After a tour in 2012, we came home to find war had broken out.

Paul and I are South Sudanese. Unfortunately politicians and their wars have destroyed much of South Sudan and taken the lives of many of our friends.

Paul: Many people lost their lives. It was a bad situation. Describing it is very hard. It can take you back into the stress.

Gordon: We came to Australia as asylum seekers. When you seek asylum, it's not because you don't love your country; it's because you have no choice.

When we first came to Australia, we didn't know anyone.

Paul: This was very hard for us. We really didn't know what to do. It's very hard to admit you are weak even though you have a strength or a talent, like we had with our music.

Gordon: We found our way to the ASRC office in Dandenong and people there helped us take classes and study English.

Paul: We attended conversation classes in a library three times a week. We would practise very simple conversations. 'Oh, you are taking tea, you are taking coffee, which one is good? How do you take it?' This helped us calm down and reduce stress step by step.

Gordon: We told the ASRC, 'We are musicians, we need to play music.'

Paul: We started performing at the ASRC in Dandenong and people kept coming back to see us. We made some connections with students who played the viola and the violin. And we formed a group, a very small group.

Paul: We then started to play music in schools and we always told the children the story of how we travelled to come here.

Gordon: People loved our music so much, and we started to compose some songs in English. The first song we composed here in Australia says: 'Stand up and clap your hands and don't keep quiet, move your body, come up here on stage with your partner. You can dance now. Show us your style, then give us your attention.'

Gordon: One of our friends said, 'I think your
music needs a band. Thom alone is not enough.'
We agreed. Paul showed them the way of the drums
and I showed them the lines of the bass and guitar –
until they knew it and we could align the rhythm.

Paul: After some time we recorded songs and uploaded
them to YouTube and found a record label. Recording
in Australia is a little bit different than in Africa. There,
people know what the music means; they understand it
on a traditional level. But it's a different culture here.
We had to teach the band everything from scratch, but
they picked it up.

Gordon: We have made over ten albums now, with the
support of friends and help from the Australian record
label Music in Exile. Our music is now popular in
Australia and we have played all around the country.'

Paul: Playing our music makes us feel good. It helped
us when we were stressed about our families or about
waiting for permanent residency.

Gordon: Seeking asylum is very difficult because you're in a new country and you need to be helped, always. You don't know where you will find a friend. We suffered a lot, but we thank God now we are Australian residents.

Paul: Life is good for us in Australia, but we miss our families. We don't know when we will see them again. They're spread around the world. We are sad that the situation in South Sudan forced us to separate from our family for such a long time. It's our dream to have all our family in one country. To have our children go to school and when they finish get a good job.

Gordon: We want to make great music. And we also want to perform for other asylum seekers – to honour then. It is very difficult to come from your country to another country, but I always tell people to remember their dreams. You've become mature, that's why you crossed the border and came from where you were to this place.

Paul: My message for other asylum seekers is: even though you are an asylum seeker, you are still a person. Think positively and try to ignore negative thoughts. Comparing your life back home to life here will only increase your stress. Making a new life is very hard, but with passion and good communication you can get to know people in the new country.

Gordon: And remember the work you used to do – this is very important. Tell people: 'In my country I used to be a lawyer, I used to be a doctor.' They will say, 'Okay, this is how we will help you.'
     When you come to seek asylum, you will need to be very patient. You need to keep quiet and wait for the government. Don't stress yourself by drinking alcohol or taking drugs. You need to be fresh in your mind. You need to have a level of patience you've never had before.

Paul: Whatever talent you come with, maybe someone here will love it and will support you and connect you with other communities. I say to people still seeking asylum: remain calm. And take whatever opportunities you have to do what you love.

Sara

When I arrived in Australia, I started working as a cultural support worker for airport arrivals. That was a wonderful job. When I saw how people smiled when they walked through the flight gates, it reminded me of how I felt when I arrived. It's an amazing feeling arriving in a new place. These smiles are pure and innocent.

I've been here ten years now, and a lot of people ask me, 'Do you still consider yourself a refugee?' There's no shame in being a refugee, but no, I'm not a refugee anymore. I'm an Australian citizen. I speak English and I've been working in this country for years.

Still, I cannot forget my old life. One day during the Brisbane Festival, I was waiting at a cafe for my morning coffee. All of a sudden, some jet planes flew overhead and I began to scream. I'd been living a stable life for fourteen years, but in two seconds my brain took me back there. I thought there was a bomb or an explosion.

Before 2003, Iraq was a very wealthy country. And Baghdad was such a beautiful place – warm weather, amazing education opportunities, and we were safe. But then the war started. Very quickly, Baghdad was completely destroyed. By 2005, Iraq had become a dangerous place. Militias started to kill people according to their sect. We left Iraq in 2006, after my neighbour, a boy the same age as me, was killed. My parents are from different sects. My mom is Shiite, and my father is Sunni. When they married, it was not a problem. But we knew we would be in trouble if the militias found out.

The only door open for Iraqis at that time was Syria. It was the summer holidays, so my dad said, 'Let's go to Syria for three months.' Well, three months ended up being six years. We couldn't get back. Month after month after month, the situation in Iraq got worse. We rented a two-bedroom unit and seven of us lived there. We couldn't work, we couldn't go to school, everything was forbidden, and over time we spent all our savings. To help us survive, the United Nations gave us a monthly food parcel.

I was trying to study my university degree remotely during this time, but it was very hard. My friend in Iraq would send me materials, but the internet in Syria was expensive. I really wanted to go back to Iraq to study but my dad said, 'No way, it's not safe.' I'm very stubborn and finally my dad agreed because I only had a short time left to complete my studies. I would live in his uncle's house, close to the university.

When I arrived, it was completely shocking. This was not the country I left nine months earlier. I saw things I'll never forgot. One day on the bus, I saw three bodies hanging from the middle of a bridge. Another time, waiting for the bus, I saw someone shot in front of me. It's been nearly twenty years, but when I close my eyes I can see it. I can still remember exactly what that man was wearing and where he was standing. I saw bodies lying in the street, and the thing was, you saw these things and you would pretend you didn't. You had to ignore it and continue on.

Before I left Syria, my dad was so worried and he warned me, 'You're going to go and you're going to die.' But I didn't care. Whatever. Let me die. I was twenty-two – not mature enough to understand death. That was, until my last day of university.

We had all been celebrating outside, taking graduation photos. We were standing at the gates of the university, waiting for our ride home. I was with my two best friends. My bus came, and I jumped in, waving goodbye. The bus had travelled less than a kilometre when suddenly a car exploded exactly where I had been standing. I lost my two closest friends that day. And in that moment, I understood what my dad meant. It was so hard. You hear about these kinds of things on the news, but when you see it in front of your eyes, it's different. I started to blame myself. Why did I leave them?

The next day I travelled back to Syria. I had succeeded, but my happiness was missing. The sound of the explosion rang in my ears. I couldn't forget it. I was no longer able to sleep – when I went to bed my heart rate was very high. I grew up very fast in a very short time.

My uncle Nasser gave us an extraordinary opportunity when he suggested we seek asylum in Australia and sponsored us. After two and half years of waiting, our visas were granted. At first we thought it was a crazy idea to go to a completely different country with a different culture and start our lives from scratch. But there was no choice. The situation in Iraq was getting worse every day. We have never regretted this decision. feel I am one of the luckiest people in the world.

My husband, Nader, has always been very supportive of me and my career. I work full-time and am about to have a third child. I could never have imagined that my life would look like this. He is always so positive and never gives up – he's very smart and always looks to the future.

I work in mental health support, and I feel very strongly about the importance of this field. We need psychologists and psychiatrists who speak our language, who understand our culture and our lived experiences. It makes such a big difference. It's a waste of time to talk to someone who doesn't speak our language and understand our culture.

I am so thankful to my uncle Nasser because through him we are now living here safely. I feel like the luckiest person in the world.

Joselyne

I was just five years old when I first learnt how to farm. Instead of going to kindergarten, my mum made a little hook for me and taught me how to dig. She gave me an area of four or five metres squared as my garden. I followed what Mum did, how she planted the seeds and put in the potatoes. When I was seven, she gave me a bigger space where I could grow my own food to sell for clothes.

We left my country, Burundi, when I was fourteen, because of civil war. People were dying. Soldiers covered in blood were killing people during the day and burning down houses at night. We couldn't take anything with us. I carried my younger sister for three days, day and night. My sides ached and we had to cross a river to get away from soldiers who were chasing us. People ran faster and faster. My feet started to swell. I could barely walk, but my mother and father were also carrying babies so there was no one to help me. It was very scary, but we survived.

We followed other refugees to a village near the border of Tanzania. The local people knew there was a war in Burundi, but they didn't have much to give us. They made maize porridge to give to the kids to survive – enough for about 2000 people. But for a week the rest of us didn't have any food. Many people became sick from malnutrition and exhaustion, and many died from diarrhea. My sisters got sick until the UNHCR brought us medication. It felt like every half an hour someone would die. We thought we were finished.

After two months, the UNHCR moved us to a camp six hours away in the middle of the bush. A truck brought food every two weeks. They gave us peas, vegetable oil, soap and a pot to cook in. The food didn't last us the whole two weeks, but we were able to survive.

After a year and a half of living in this camp, we wanted something to do. We didn't have any money so we swapped food with people in Tanzania in exchange for land to grow food. There were bad people living between the village and the refugee camp – they would beat or kill people, steal from them and rape women and girls. If you needed to go to the village, you never knew if you would make it back to the camp or not.

I started secondary school at eighteen. To study we had to wear shoes, but my parents didn't have any money to buy them, so I wore thongs. After they broke, my teacher said, 'Go home until you get more shoes.' I don't know how my dad did it, but two days later I had shoes and was able to go back.

I lived in the camp for twelve years and finished high school there when I was about twenty-three or twenty-four. Two years later, I got married.

I came to Australia with my partner in 2005. I left my parents and younger siblings behind. My partner and I applied for settlement overseas because there was nothing to go back to in Burundi. One day they told us we had been chosen to go to Australia. At school I'd seen Australia on the map – it looked like it was at the end of the world. I was so scared, I felt like it was somewhere you would go to die.

When we arrived in Australia, we were taken to a transition house, where some old people had cooked us food. Apart from bananas, we didn't recognise the food at all, so we didn't touch it. A young Kenyan boy tried to explain everything, but we didn't touch the food on the table for four days – we didn't think it was for us. We weren't able to cook because we didn't know how to use the stove. We had a vacuum cleaner, but we didn't know how to use it. It was all so unfamiliar.

On the first night we were too scared to sleep; we thought the white people would come and eat us. Back home we were afraid of white people. We thought they were dangerous – demons. But the next day we realised that since these people had given us food they must be good people. So on the second night we slept.

We spent three months in the transition house and then moved to a house where we could live by ourselves, practising what we had learnt.

After a year in Newcastle, I approached an organisation to help bring my parents, sisters and brothers to Australia. I had a broken heart. I would start crying all the time because I missed my friends and family. So I asked them to help my family settle here. After two years, in 2008, my family came to Australia.

In 2012, we moved to Mildura. We didn't have anywhere to farm at first but we persisted in trying to find our own land. Three years ago our dreams became true. Now we are part of a cooperative called Food Next Door. It matches famers like me with land that is not being used. Now we spend most of our free time growing our food, sharing our knowledge with the community, teaching the children and working the soil.

I grow beans and peanuts, spinach, big white African eggplants, amaranth, beetroot, watermelon, sweet potato and many other things. I couldn't buy maize anywhere – so I began to grow it. Maize is my favourite to eat. It clears my heart and puts me in a good mood.

I love farming. You get to work with the soil and eat fresh food. A mentor showed us how to grow food here in Australia organically. We don't use any chemicals – we feed the soil instead. And we don't need to go to the gym. Gardening gives your feet life.

Before I moved here, we didn't know anyone, but now I have met so many different people – other farmers and visitors. Through the farm, I feel like part of the community.

'The farm means many things to me.
No farm, no food. No food, no life.
You can't live a healthy life without
healthy food. So you need farms producing
healthy food.'

Joselyne

Thanush

It feels like someone has sliced open my neck and I have not yet died. Every day is incredibly painful.

We are innocent. We sought asylum, but instead of being given safety we were punished. For eight years I was held in detention. We were never told when we would be released. We were separated from our families. For months at a time we were locked inside, unable to feel the sun on our skin.

Now some of us are outside. But we are suffering on temporary visas. There is no certainty in our future. We cannot endure any more pain. We want to be free.

I have never really had a permanent home. When I was a child in Sri Lanka, we were always on the move because of the war. Thousands of innocent Tamil people were murdered. Not long after the government announced that any Tamil person could be arrested without reason, my parents told me I needed to leave: 'Anywhere you live, we will be happy. So long as you are alive. That's all we need.'

I was twenty years old and alone when I left my country. I registered with the United Nations High Commissioner for Refugees in Malaysia. They interviewed me and recognised me as a refugee. But their recognition didn't give me anything except a card that said I was a 'refugee'. I had no citizenship, no passport, no support and no options for building a life.

I came to Australia by boat. We were seeking safety. I thought they were welcoming us when we arrived. I thought I would be able to start my new life. I believed my dreams would come true.

We were separated into two groups. One group of people were kept on Christmas Island and eventually they were sent to Australia; the other group was exiled to Manus Island in Papua New Guinea. To this day we don't know on what basis they chose the two groups.

I was among those transferred to Manus. The UNHCR rules state that it should only take a maximum of six months to process a refugee application. I spent eight years in detention.

The first of us to die was Reza Barati. We carried him to the gates and begged the guards to take him for emergency medical treatment. He did not get treatment. His body lay waiting at the gates for hours. The next day we found out he had died.

These are the names of the fourteen men who died in Australia's offshore detention system.

Reza Barati

Sayed Ibrahim Hussein

Hamid Kehazaei

Omid Masoumali

Rakib Khan

Kamil Hussain

Faysal Ishak Ahmed

Hamed Shamshiripour

Rajeev Rajendran

Jahingir

Salim Kyawning

Fariborz Karami

Sayed Mirwais Rohani

Abdirahman Ahmed Mohammed

Year after year, I watched my friends die. They lost their lives and their futures waiting for freedom. We screamed but our screams were not heard.

Every morning I woke up with one dream in my mind – my only dream, which is freedom. But when I thought about my situation, tears fell from my eyes. Day after day, my situation remained unchanged. I didn't have any solution to release my pain.

We had no control over our lives or our bodies. Even criminals know the length of their sentence, but in our case we were detained indefinitely.

They chose to forget that we are human beings, not border protection tools.

After six years of unbearable pain, I attempted suicide by taking an overdose of pills. Because of this, I was transferred to the Mantra hotel prison in Preston, Melbourne. I was expecting better conditions there than in PNG – perhaps I would finally get the mental health care that I needed to recover. Instead, they kept me inside a hotel room for nine months. Without sunlight on my skin or fresh air in my lungs. How did being locked in a room help me?

I tried to hang myself in that room. I felt that the only way I could be free was suicide. I could not find any other way to end the pain of my suffering. Now I knew how my friends on Manus who had taken their lives must have felt. My roommate found me unconscious; he saved my life.

I have survived to this day because of the love from thousands of wonderful Australian friends who have supported us through this suffering. Their protests speak truth to power; they have touched our lives with compassion. We would be dead without them.

Thanush selvarasa @Thanus79084726 · May 30, 2019 ···

After haveing going through with unbearable pain for the last 6yrs. I found
the only way for my freedom is death. I couldn't find any other ways to get
rid of my pain but death eventhough security didn't let it happen & want me
to continue with my pain forever. #freedom #Manus

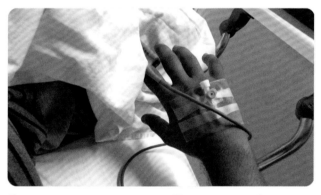

○ 15   ⊔ 69   ♡ 38   ⬆

'We screamed but our screams were not heard.'

Thanush

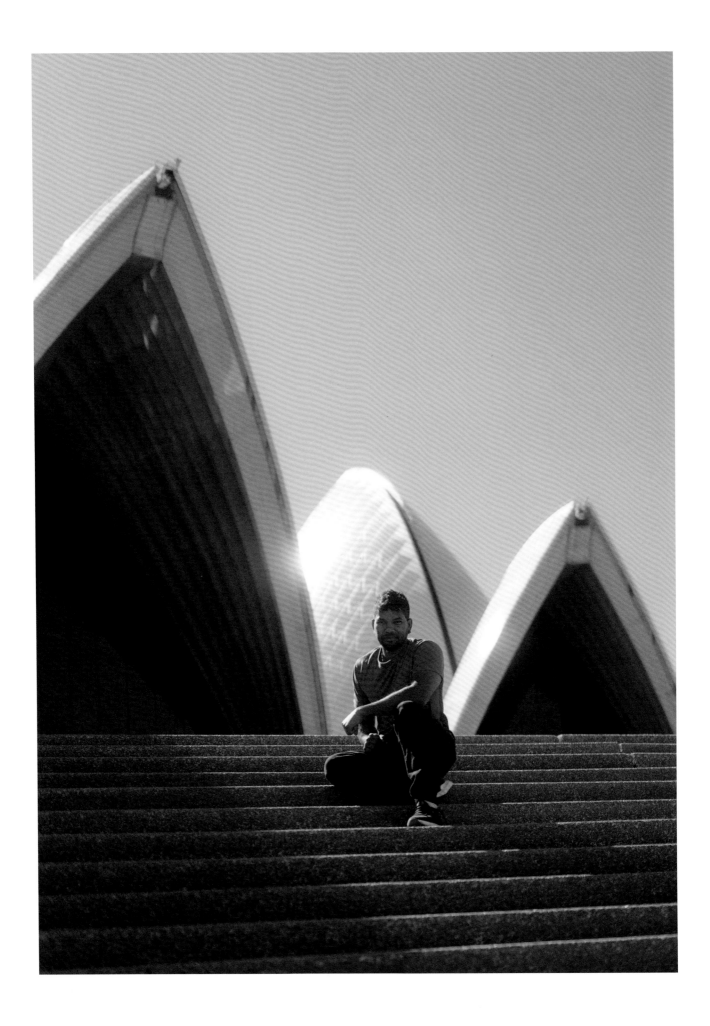

In the past few months since my 'release', I have got my drivers licence, forklift licence and white card for construction work. I am now working as a disability support worker. I help people with their cooking or draw pictures with them. I also work at a supermarket, loading and unloading stock.

My dream is to build a home in Australia. To make a family and have a peaceful life. I want to start a business and build a future here. I haven't seen my parents for twelve years and I miss them so much. I would love to see them. Although some of us have been 'released' from detention, many of my friends are still imprisoned indefinitely. Even for those of us who have been 'released', our Temporary Protection Visas offer no certainty. I have been to Canberra to talk with politicians and I've held the megaphone at protests. I will not stop until every one of my friends has found what they came here for: permanent safety and freedom.

Every weekend I go to a new place in Sydney and try to relax my mind and forget about my past. I want to celebrate my happiness.

We cannot endure any more pain. We want to be free.

Susan

Ballarat and its cold weather remind me a little bit of Nepal: of Kathmandu, where I went to school and college. When I cook Nepalese food, I feel a bit like I'm back home. I make momos and Nepalese noodles almost every weekend.

I used to be a teacher back in Nepal and I'm a childcare educator now. I love my job: even when I'm really missing my own daughter and son, I give one hundred per cent love to the children I'm looking after.

I had to leave my first two children in Nepal with my parents. My daughter was just six months old when I left; she really misses me. Whenever she sees other parents with their babies, she asks why we are not together.

In Nepal, my husband was involved in politics: when the Maoist Party took over the leadership of our country, after a civil war, they targeted people who opposed them. My husband was one of them. They asked us for donations. We paid a lot of money for many years to protect our lives. But it was very hard because we didn't have that much income. But if we didn't pay, they could kill us. So we decided we must leave.

In 2011, we decided to go to India. The border was nearby and I spoke Hindi. I was twenty-two, my eldest son was nearly four and we also had a newborn baby – just eleven days old.

In India, we suffered a lot. We moved from one place to another, but we didn't feel safe anywhere. Even in India, the Maoists could easily discover where we were. We also found out that Nepalese women are not safe in India. I became very ill from stress and poor nutrition. I went to a doctor, who said he would help, but he abused me. The police didn't believe me. We had no one there. We felt so hopeless and helpless. We couldn't turn to anyone for help.

My husband and I decided that while we could survive without much food and in hard conditions, the kids couldn't. Not knowing where we would end up, we left our son and daughter with my mum and dad in India. I am so sad about that now.

We flew to Singapore because Nepalese people can get an arrival visa there. But we didn't find any hope there – it is a nice country but we had little money and couldn't survive living there illegally. After a week we travelled to Malaysia by bus. We went to the UNHCR to apply for asylum, but they told us that Malaysia doesn't accept people from Nepal.

I sat down in the street nearby and sobbed. I missed my children, I missed my home. There was no way for us to return to Nepal safely, and we had no idea what to do next. We had no hope left. My husband and I even considered ending our lives.

A man came up to us on the street and told us about a boat going to Australia. It felt like God had sent an angel. I know people call him a people smuggler, but in my opinion he saved our lives.

We paid him a lot of money and he arranged everything for us. It was a really scary time. We travelled to Indonesia and they took us to the jungle, where we stayed in a small hotel room. We thought maybe we would be left there for years and no one would find us. They brought only a small piece of chicken and rice to eat each day. We don't eat meat, so my husband and I survived on rice.

After twenty-two days they said it was time to go. We walked through the jungle to a small boat. There were sixty-two people and ten babies aboard. It was my first experience of the ocean; I had never seen it before, as Nepal is a landlocked country.

We spent nearly seven days in that small boat. No toilet, no safety equipment, not much food, nothing. After three days, we ran out of water. Finally a Singapore navy vessel approached us. They said, 'You are going the wrong way to get to Australia and there is a big storm coming. If you keep going that way, you will disappear.' They said, 'If you survive until morning, go this way and the Indonesian or Australian navy will find you. But you may not survive.' People started crying and praying. In the night, the storm was huge. Our boat was flying up to the sky and crashing back down again. It took on water and almost sank. As the sun came up the Australian navy rescued us.

When I tell this story, all the memories come back …

My husband and I spent nearly fifteen months in detention centres near Darwin. They threatened us and tried to send us back to Nepal many times. They told us we didn't have a strong case. Sometimes they said they'd give us money and buy a house in India for us. They asked why we didn't go to India. There was a lot of mental pressure on us.

When I became pregnant with my third child, they moved us to detention in Victoria. When I was in a detention centre in Ballarat, the local people, particularly members of Rural Australians for Refugees, helped a lot. They visited every week and I came to know them well.

Once we were released from the Melbourne detention centre in 2014, we went to Ballarat to work regionally. I love the community here.

I have now been officially found to be a refugee – but I only have a five-year visa. We can't get permanent protection and there is no option for family reunion. Right now, there is no pathway for permanent protection for us. The only way we could stay in Australia permanently is if we divorced and remarried Australian citizens. We can't do that. Our two children who were born in Australia are stateless, because they were born in detention centres.

'I just want a safe life
in Australia
with my whole
family together.'

Susan

I love my work and am studying for a diploma. I am very happy here, but my life is in limbo because I don't have my children. If I had a magic wand and could change one thing in Australia, I would see every refugee family reunited.

I just want a safe life in Australia with my whole family together.

Every night I dream of having all my children together. I hope that one day I'll be reunited with them.

Daytime is easy because I keep my mind busy. But at night I can't sleep because I am so worried about my kids. I don't know when I will see them again. We talk every day. I try to keep very involved in their lives. We do homework together on the phone and I check that they are really brushing their teeth properly. Being in this limbo makes me question what I am doing with my life. It's so hard to not give up. My children give me strength.

Since I have come to Australia I have been on antidepressants. My mental health is ruined. Rather than taking these pills I need my children.

Flora

My home is like a two-way mirror,

a single-sided reflection on each side.

On days when my sickness for my home takes over me,

I don't know which side I belong to.

I wonder: is it this side of home I belong to, or the other?

How can it be that I am homesick for a place that may be foreign to me?

Despite everything about me being visible on each side of the mirror –

the sides that don't quite fit right,

the sides that don't sound right,

quick or sharp enough at the tip of my tongue,

the sides that I may have to grind down fine

or hide to fit in on this side of home.

My home is like a two-way mirror,

a distant memory that may be too far away to reach

but is a part of me although I may forget that it exists.

Memories of my home tell me that it hurts to be here.

It hurts to belong – and home should never hurt.

But if you're reminded each day that you do not belong,

you may be in the right place at the wrong time,

and the pain it brings to your heart may even transcend a lifetime.

When day comes, things will cease to hurt anymore.

I will slick my hair back in my grandmother's shea nut oil

while the sun's rays melt the oil down my scalp,

down the grooves of my neck to the slopes of my back.

Aunty would part my hair to braid it, the gentle hands that raised me

securing each strand of my hair and every inch of my being that was once astray.

Lost in a labyrinth of false hopes and ambitions,

bottled up in a glass house, I will come back to me –

back to the home of my body,

the home I have fought to evict myself from to save myself from the pain within.

The tears of my soul will form an endless stream

that will one day reach God.

And God will tell me that only I can drink from the cup of my own misery,

and only I can turn my tears into seeds and nourish the soil of my body.

My home is like a two-way mirror

where the tea doesn't taste like twigs dancing in bland water

but of love and inner peace.

My aunty would wake before the fat rooster's alarm,

the kettle would whistle on wood log flames,

we would all sit beneath the canopy of the hut my uncle built,

drink tea that's too sweet to be tea,

creating memories of home that will last a lifetime,

no matter which side of home we may belong to.

Aheda

I have two secrets for cooking. The first is not my secret but my country's: 'Cook with your hands.' The second is love. You need to put some love in your cooking.

I've been cooking my whole life. In Palestine I was a chef and I ran a catering business. All my favourite recipes come from my grandmother and her grandmother. I need to hold onto them and share them. These recipes are my culture and I want my culture to continue.

Our land is very old. My family has lived in Palestine for many generations – thousands of years.

In 1948 Israel began to violently force Palestinian people from their home – about half the population either fled or was murdered. This was the beginning of Nakba, which means 'catastrophe'. In 1967 my big brother carried me, a two-year-old girl, on his shoulders from our home in Palestine across to Jordan. For two days he walked without food and water. When we chat now on the phone, he likes to joke about how strong we were, how we held on to life. We lived in a tent with thousands of other Palestinians for two years before we could return to our village.

The blood of my family has been soaked into these lands by the guns of soldiers. I have many hard stories. When my home was taken as a child. When my white Mitsubishi Lancer was kneaded like dough by a tank. When my home was taken again – when I had children of my own – and converted into a police station.

My children who could escape are now scattered across the world. I live alone, without my children, my land or my culture. Everything I had has been taken from me.

Israel is still hurting Palestinian people. There are more than seven million Palestinian refugees worldwide; this is more than from any other country. They live in refugee camps, as stateless people in Iraq, Jordan, Egypt and Lebanon – or in countries like Australia, far removed from our language and culture. The Palestinians who remain in our land live in fear.

It's very hard to watch and I wish more people would pay attention to the truth.

Here in Australia I feel safe. When I take the bus or walk in the street or park, I am safe.

I am happiest in my garden. Every day I wake up, make coffee and chat with my plants. I ask them how they are feeling: 'Do you need something? Some food? Some water?' It is a very happy place for me. In summer I have zucchini and eggplant ready. When you cook Palestinian food, the vegetables must be fresh because it's very simple. For my mother's baba ganoush, you smoke the eggplant on a flame, then add lemon, salt, garlic and tahina. That's it. I like to keep it classic, the same as my grandmother.

It has not always been easy in Australia. When I arrived four years ago I couldn't speak any English. I could only say 'yes' or 'no'. Now I run cooking courses for people to learn my Palestinian recipes.

My dream is to open up a food truck called Aheda's Kitchen. I want to travel around Australia sharing Palestinian food. When people try my dishes and say, 'Oh my gosh, that's so delicious', it makes me feel proud.

I miss my home. I miss my country. I miss my family. I can never go back to Palestine but I will always be Palestinian. I hope and pray that one day Palestine will be free.

'I miss my home. I miss my country. I miss my family. I can never go back to Palestine but I will always be Palestinian. I hope and pray that one day Palestine will be free.'

Aheda

Abdul

When we come together through cricket, we are like a family. Where you are from – your religion, race or culture – doesn't matter. We started the All Nations Social Cricket team as a way for people seeking asylum, who often feel isolated in the community, to make new friendships. Most of the players in our team have endured tough times, but when we come together we don't have to face that hardship alone.

We began with some old bats and gloves with holes in them. It didn't matter: we played with passion. Our team is about more than cricket, but that doesn't mean we don't play to win. We train hard; even in winter we practise every week in the nets.

Like me, some of the people on our team have been waiting years for permanent protection visas. My wife and I have been seeking asylum in Australia since 2013. We came here for safety – we didn't know that there was another journey waiting for us.

For the past eleven-and-a-half years we have been surviving under difficult visa conditions. We have no work rights, no Centrelink, we're not allowed to study, and we don't have access to Medicare. We feel like we are being held in a cage.

We try to keep positive, but we are human. If you compare our bodies to when we arrived in Australia, we look very different. Our physical and mental health has suffered so much.

After a few years of living like this, my wife nearly took her own life. She has a Master's in political science, but without any opportunities to work or hope of things changing she gave up. I thank God that she survived. The ASRC organised with the hospital to ensure we could get treatment without a Medicare card. This was the turning point for me. As my wife started to recover, I wanted to say thank you not just in words, but with actions.

So I started volunteering at the Monash Health Community Centre. I help patients, particularly those in wheelchairs, by showing them the way to their treatments and appointments. I also spend a lot of time just chatting and offering support.

One day I was talking to a guy in his fifties in the dialysis ward. I would often talk to the people on this ward because they have to wait there for four to five hours at a time. He asked me, 'What do you do?' I mentioned that I run a cricket program for asylum seekers and refugees. And he replied with some very insensitive things. He was pretty cold with me.

Every week I went back to try to sit with him. He saw that I was volunteering, and eventually I got a chance to tell him my story. His attitude totally changed. It wasn't through debate or arguing that I changed his mind; it was through my actions as a volunteer.

'Don't give up, give back' is my motto. It's even printed on our cricket jerseys. It's by giving back rather than giving up that I am in the headspace I am in today. I've gone from victim to victor. We have lost so much talent and skill in Australia because people are isolated from their communities. And I have witnessed this drive people to suicide. People seeking asylum often feel disconnected and lonely because they are denied their basic human rights. They might be living in Australia, they might be your neighbour, but they are living in a different 'zone' because of their visa conditions.

That's part of why this cricket club exists. It's an opportunity for people to make friends and feel connected to their new community. To find strength and solidarity together. Last year our team won the Melbourne Champions League and we went on to play the Aussie Champion League on the Gold Coast. We've hosted teams from all over the country here in Dandenong for the 'Don't Give Up, Give Back Cup'. I am so proud of what we have achieved, but I want to take it even further.

Every year my wife and I hope that next year will be better. Day after day we are worn down. We still don't know where we will end up. Will it be another eleven years of pain?

Many refugees have got permanent residency but remain deeply scarred from the trauma and stress of living in limbo. By the time we get to call Australia home, will we be completely ruined physically and mentally? This is what worries me the most.

A lot of things in this world aren't going great: we all know that. But I say if we want change to happen then we have to bring people together. We have to smile for each other and cry for each other.

We all have to be more active and work together to make this world more beautiful – with love, peace and humanity.

Every day I live my motto: Don't give up, give back!

Abdul

Amparo

One fine day, operating difficulties, excessive taxes and 'vaccines' (illegally extorted payments in exchange for protection or permission to keep operating) brought the company where I worked for nineteen years to bankruptcy. The livelihood of hundreds of families in the area suddenly vanished. I could think of only one way to survive: I would start a new business, a fast-food restaurant, in my town, Gómez Plata, Antioquia, in the north of Colombia.

I set up the restaurant 10 metres from a military base of the National Army of Colombia, without realising this would upset one of the National Liberation Army (ELN) fronts, a group founded on far-left ideals and involved in ongoing armed conflict in Colombia. They unleashed a hail of threats against my family and me. First, it was a visit from a man who put an arm around my neck, then threatening phone calls, and finally a bomb threat. These events ended up making me flee from the town where I was born, grew up and had lived all my life.

There was no justice or state power that could protect me. Despite making complaints and going through all the avenues for help the Colombian state provides, all I received was a piece of advice: No dé papaya – a Colombian expression meaning 'don't give someone the opportunity to take advantage of you'.

So I wondered: *what do you do when not even the police can protect you?*

Then my own husband, the father of my daughters and the man with whom I had spent more than thirty years, informed me that he was leaving me for another woman. I had always been taught that as a woman I must turn a blind eye to my husband's affairs to keep him happy. Even though I did so, he still left me. I was heartbroken.

I ended up displaced in the city of Medellin, couchsurfing with my relatives. 'At least now I am safe,' I thought. How wrong I was.

The claws of war reached me in Medellin: twice when I left my nieces' homes, I was approached by ELN guerrilla fighters in the middle of the street. The order had been given that I had to leave their territory. After those encounters and driven by severe depression and fear, I began to consider taking my own life.

Either I would give up living, or I would somehow find the strength to invent a new life for myself. God sent me a gift to help me choose the second option: I received news that a grandson was coming, the son of my youngest daughter, Juliana, who lived in Australia.

So in complete secrecy and with the generous help of my closest family, we raised funds so that I could travel to Australia on a tourist visa to support Juli in her pregnancy and the birth of my grandson.

One has to forgive in order to live.

I arrived in Australia on 17 September 2019 – on that day I was born again. This place is quiet, peaceful. Here, people are not afraid that the door will be kicked in any second by someone wanting to kill you.

Months after arriving and on the advice of Juli's mother-in-law (who came to Australia as a refugee from Central America in the 1970s), we went to an immigration lawyer. I discovered that there was a thing called a 'refugee visa' and that I could seek asylum in Australia given that my life would be in danger if I returned to Colombia.

I didn't really understand what a refugee was, but here I am today: a lady on a provisional refugee visa who dreams of becoming an elegant Australian señora who goes to Mass on Sundays, works, and speaks English. Meanwhile, I will continue doing my favourite thing: exploring this beautiful city. I'll keep taking my little boy to the park and talking to other women even if I do not understand them much. The most difficult thing about being here is not knowing much English, but I hope that later on I can go to a college to study the language and then meet more people my age.

This country is wonderful, and I am very grateful it took me in to protect me from the nightmare I lived through; I love Australia very much. And don't get me wrong, my Colombia is so beautiful, but also so unjust with so much war, violence and poverty – that it is an immense struggle just to live day by day.

Can you imagine being able to bring people in Colombia those good mattresses that people here throw away? That would be a great joy!

Meanwhile, so as not to miss my country so much, I keep listening to vallenatos, Colombian folk music, and cooking my Colombian food, my paisa tray, my sancocho and all the food that makes me feel like I'm at home, in a little Colombia.

Australia cured my heart of so much resentment and so much sadness and allowed me to become a new Amparo. I overcame so many difficulties, and I am still here telling the story. I am still a quiet person, but I'm not shy, and I've never stopped being kind and generous with my people. Here, many young people from the Colombian community see me as their mother in the distance.

I decided to forgive the violent people who took my place in the world from me, just as I also had to forgive my ex-husband in order to move on. One has to forgive in order to live; if you don't, you only see your past and miss what's in front of you.

I cry telling this story, but many of these tears are ones of pride in myself.

'One has to forgive in order to live.'

Amparo

Part Three

The ASRC Story

Letter from Kon

Little has been written about the humble beginnings of the Asylum Seeker Resource Centre – but it's a tale I've told many times. It's the story of how the ASRC started as a TAFE class project for a group of students I was teaching in Footscray, students who were passionate about and committed to social justice but who couldn't find a local charity that would take them on for a community placement. So we decided to create our own.

The idea of the ASRC was born out of the principles that everyone has a right to help and that as a community we should share what we can – so we started with food.

In a small shopfront, no larger than your average living room, with a few buckets of paint and some odd bits of furniture, we lined the shelves full with whatever food we could find, and the ASRC was born – on 8 June 2001.

In the twenty years since then, thousands of people have walked through our doors and we continued to be a loud and persistent voice for change, and at the coalface offered countless support services where people need us most.

We talk about 'hope' often at the ASRC. It's in the very fabric of who we are, woven through our history and inscribed on the walls of our building. In the beginning, when this was all just a dream, hope is what powered us. And it's what keeps us going today.

I'm proud of that, and grateful to everyone who has been part of our journey of hope and who has helped us create this community of compassion and welcome – to every person who has supported our work in whichever way they could, to each volunteer who rolled up their sleeves. And to the movement of people across this country who stand with people seeking asylum, on the right side of history, and say 'the way people are being treated is wrong, and we can – and must – do better'.

The work the ASRC has done over twenty years has been built upon the hopes of thousands of people who have come here seeking safety.

In the early days we used to record the names of everyone we helped in blue notebooks. We stopped using the books in 2012, as the volume of people we were working with had increased so much. But had we continued, the names would be more than 20,000 now.

Twenty thousand people – each with their own experience of seeking asylum, their own unique story. These are stories that all Australians should hear. Just like the stories in this book you hold in your hands.

Many of the people we helped are now settled in Australia, while many continue to navigate the arduous protection process. Given the same opportunities as us all, they have gone on to live their lives in peace and safety. People who left the ASRC with protection have come back to visit years later, proudly telling us of the family they now have or the business they have built. Some have become powerful voices for change, community leaders who represent the very best of what we can be as a society. People who with tenacity and strength have survived and who speak truth to power.

It's an honour and a privilege to work with refugees – courageous, resilient and resourceful people, who love their families so deeply they cross the Earth to find sanctuary and safety here. What everyone deserves as human beings is the right to be protected, live in safety and with freedom. And that includes the right for voices to be heard.

These stories speak to what an inclusive and welcoming Australia can look like for us all – one of hope, inclusion, compassion, belonging, equality and welcome. For everyone.

And through sharing our stories with each other, we can find unity in what makes us different.

Kon Karapanagiotidis OAM
CEO & Founder, Asylum Seeker Resource Centre

Twenty Years of Hope

When the ASRC opened its doors on 8 June 2001, refugees and people seeking asylum weren't used as political weapons, as they are today, to spark debate about borders and national security. But just a few months after the first families received food donations from a small but bustling ASRC shopfront 'filled with hope', the discourse around refugees in Australia changed overnight.

In October 2001, in the wake of the *Tampa* affair and having refused to let refugees rescued at sea land in Australia, Prime Minister John Howard stated, 'We will decide who comes to Australia and the circumstances in which they come.' It marked a seismic, and shameful shift in Australia's refugee policies.

Over the next twenty years, successive governments have demonised and dehumanised people seeking asylum, people who are simply seeking safety and a chance to rebuild their lives in peace with their families. Political point-scoring and arbitrary policy changes have only caused further harm.

But there was good reason for hope, because a groundswell of people began standing together to say enough is enough. As Kon Karapangiotidis observed at the tenth anniversary of the ASRC in 2011, something changed post-Tampa in the consciousness of the Australian public.

People suddenly felt differently – there was a level of anger and outrage at how people were treated. So many times, I heard from complete strangers that became new friends: 'I've got to do something. I can't stand what's being done in my name.' And that outrage has continued to this day.'

Kon Karapanagiotidis, founder and CEO

And so, very quickly, the ASRC grew into something more.

In 2002, the Centre, still then just a shopfront providing food aid, became a legal clinic providing advice for people in their claims for protection – this is now known as the Human Rights Law Program, a community legal centre. Kon and his sister Nola led an army of willing volunteers – many turning up after hours and taking on as many cases as they could in the evenings. In those early days, many applications were submitted for people who had learnt of the ASRC only after their application had been unfairly rejected. Many appeals on-merit were lodged, and within the first years of operation cases were even heard before a sitting judge of the High Court.

As word spread that the ASRC was distributing food to those who needed it, people started turning up seeking other forms of support. Navigating the refugee determination process and gaining access to support is far from straightforward, and back then it was next to impossible. Thus began the ASRC's Casework Program.

Sherrine Clark, one of the original students in the class project that founded the ASRC and now Director of Humanitarian Services, recalls that at the time the mantra was: do what we can to help with whatever resources are available.

There were no mainstream services that really supported people seeking asylum in an informed way – they did their best, but at the time, we were the psychosocial support and crisis intervention response for people who just needed someone to turn to. And while the work was complex, the idea was simple. People would turn up, they had an issue, we'd listen and in whatever way possible we'd find a solution.

Sherrine Clark, Director of Humanitarian Services

There was something unique about the energy within the ASRC.

I remember fondly those early years, when Heidi, our community development coordinator, would put on a theatre production with members – it made everyone happy, despite the trauma that was such a significant part of peoples' lives. Despite the challenges everyone was facing, there were a lot of smiles and laughter and kindness.

Sherrine Clark, Director of Humanitarian Services

Out of the questions asked of the ASRC in those early years grew some of the Centre's most profound work, helping people not just survive but thrive. As it expanded, renting a vacant office above its bustling foodbank, someone asked whether the ASRC might run English language classes. So began the Education Program – within weeks it was helping people learn English.

That mantra stuck – whenever people seeking asylum asked the ASRC if they could help, the answer was 'we'll find a way'. Even if money was tight (and for many years it was) or they didn't immediately have the resources, Kon, his students and the growing group of volunteers found a way.

The foodbank grew into a mini kitchen that could provide a hot meal.

It's quite special, with food cooked from around the world – by people who may not speak a word of English but who communicate through the universal language of food. For a moment everyone has a seat at the table, together, as equals.

Kon Karapanagiotidis, founder and CEO

Some of the people eating those meals asked where they might go for medicine and health care, providing the impetus to set up the ASRC Health Clinic, which opened in April 2002, supported by volunteer doctors and nurses.

By 2004, the ASRC had outgrown its beginnings on Nicholson Street, Footscray. More than 1000 people each year were coming to the ASRC for assistance. It opened up an outpost in West Melbourne, and another in Thornbury, where it would soon start ASRC Catering, a place where people seeking asylum could obtain their first job in Australia. The same year, the ASRC began building job pathways through the Employment Program.

From its earliest days, the ASRC established a commitment to political advocacy and campaigning for justice. With churches, community groups and the refugee sector, it campaigned for the development of community detention, allowing families who had been incarcerated to live in the community while their applications were processed. At the same time, campaigning to end 'detention debt' so people weren't leaving detention owing up to tens of thousands of dollars. The ASRC's advocacy work has been instrumental in shining a spotlight on the inhumane conditions and destabilising effects of indefinite detention.

2007 saw an end to offshore mandatory detention, but the harm suffered by those who endured this cruelty was immense: many people were released into the community with significant trauma. That year, the West Melbourne Centre became the official home of the ASRC. It would remain so until 2014, when the Centre got a permanent 'Home of Hope', just 30 metres down the road from where the ASRC originally began in Footscray, more than a decade earlier.

By 2012, the ASRC opened its second social enterprise, ASRC Cleaning, furthering pathways to employment.

In 2013, the ASRC received its largest donation to support advocacy and attitude change. Thanks to the donation, we partnered with Republic of Everyone and Heckler to launch the Hot Potato – where the ASRC visited ten towns in ten days, serving up 10,000 potatoes, countless conversations and the production of a documentary, Road to Transformation. The project aimed to build common understanding, challenge political propaganda and encourage people to reassess the ways in which Australia could support people seeking asylum.

By late 2014 the ASRC had begun a new approach to service design, known as 'symbiotic innovation', whereby solutions to challenges are community-led. The ASRC's Innovation Hub opened in 2015, with a rallying cry of 'change starts now'. Founding Director Gavin Ackerley noted that people seeking asylum 'don't need handouts, but a hand up'. The old agency model needed to evolve and change would have to come from grassroots organisations such as the ASRC.

The dream was to create this space that's not about being a person seeking asylum but about being everything else. Being an artist, a musician, an engineer… about what went before and what's going to come and all those aspirations.

Gavin Ackerley, former Director of the Innovation Hub

With activities including a women's program, excursions and immersion activities for young people, music and sports groups, community-led events and entrepreneurship services, the ASRC had expanded its capacity to support people to thrive and have self-determination of their futures.

It's about more than restoring income, it's about people's agency. Their empowerment and independence so that they have the tools they need to succeed – the ASRC is just part of their journey. But together, we can build hope and transform lives.

Abiola Ajetomobi, Director of the Innovation Hub

In late 2014, the pathway to permanent protection became increasingly difficult for people who arrived in Australia by boat. Temporary Protection Visas were introduced, leaving thousands of the ASRC's clients in limbo. In this process, known as 'Fast Track', the government amended Australia's refugee status determination processes, meaning people who arrived by boat without a valid visa were no longer eligible for permanent protection; this affected 24,500 people.

In early 2017, many of these people were suddenly given a new deadline by which their applications must be submitted, resulting in the ASRC's legal program processing some 791 new applications for protection in the space of mere months to meet a deadline of 1 October. At the time the ASRC's lawyers usually fielded about 200 new applications for protection each year. It was an unprecedented moment in the refugee sector and the ASRC's legal team rose to the challenge.

Late in 2017, the government's Status Resolution Support Services (SRSS), which provided people with a small payment to cover basic needs and allowed them to access health services while they sought asylum, began to be removed. SRSS was a crucial lifeline for many and as it was removed the number of people the ASRC supported annually increased rapidly to more than 6000.

> I noticed almost overnight that there were more children in the Centre, lining up with their parents. Families with children as young as six were being cut off and left to fend for themselves.
>
> *Kon Karapanagiotidis, founder and CEO*

For the first time in our history, we acquired sleeping bags for people to use if they needed to sleep rough, as the demand for our housing program had skyrocketed. We were concerned we wouldn't be able to meet the demand, and this was our only option.

> *Sherrine Clark, Director of Humanitarian Services*

In 2016 ASRC staff visited Christmas Island, and in 2017 Manus Island, to bear witness and report on the conditions faced by those in Australia's arbitrary offshore detention. Jana Favero, Director of Campaigns & Advocacy, recalls the incredible spirit and resilience of the men they met there.

> Visiting Manus is something I will never forget. Seeing men we had spoken to on the phone countless times gave all of us even more motivation to work on 'searing advocacy' in their name. In understanding the horrific maze that is the system of offshore processing, there is no substitute for seeing it with your own eyes.
>
> *Jana Favero, Director of Campaigns & Advocacy*

In mid-2018, the ASRC joined a coalition of refugee and humanitarian organisations in a campaign to see all children on Nauru and their families medically evacuated to Australia. At the start of the campaign over 100 children were trapped on Nauru. Thanks to a groundswell of public support and crossbench and cross party political pressure, less than 6 months later all children (and their families) were flown from Nauru to Australia.

In 2019, Blueprint for Free Speech gave a Special Recognition Award to the ASRC for its work with whistleblowers exposing conditions on Nauru and other offshore detention centres. On the back of the success of Kids Off Nauru, public and private advocacy saw men and women medically evacuated to Australia after the passing of Medevac legislation.

The passing of the Medevac legislation is a milestone moment as it gives us a glimpse of what we can be as a country and society. Where people seeking asylum are treated fairly, with dignity and offered the safety and protection they deserve. It's quite something that the first time a government has lost a vote on its own legislation in decades was a bill about refugees.

Jana Favero, Director of Campaigns & Advocacy

At the heart of all this work – whatever form it took – were people seeking asylum driving change and honouring us by sharing their stories of hardship, resilience and courage.

When I first discovered the Asylum Seeker Resource Centre, I thought of myself as a victim. Things in my life were not going well and my wife needed urgent medical care for a breast tumour. The health team at the ASRC were able to find a solution, and over the years the ASRC has supported us in many other ways. There have been periods when we would have been homeless if we didn't have them on our side. Because of the love I was shown, I decided that instead of giving up on life I would give back. That's why I started the cricket team and I have been volunteering once a week in the ASRC foodbank for years now. I come and get my groceries for the week here and I give my time to help out in the centre.

Abdul

I came here in 2008 and got my protection visa in 2015. In that time, ASRC provided me with all types of support: for my mental health, legal representation, food, a job at ASRC Cleaning. But they also gave me so much more than these things. They believed in me, gave me courage to live and they understood what I was going through. I used to finish work every day and go home sad. Now I am here, smiling, happy. God sends you to good people when you are in trouble and God sent me to the ASRC. Now I have permanent protection in Australia, and I am running my own business. Because I am safe, I can support my family, including my son who I haven't seen since he was a baby. I survived, and I want to help another generation survive. The ASRC helped give me my life back. And not only mine, but thousands behind me and in front of me.

Mohamed

It's for people like Abdul and Mohamed that the ASRC needed to raise money, to ensure the support they needed was available. In the early days that looked like Kon hosting a stand-up comedy night to raise just enough to keep the doors open – the Centre was built off the back of lemonade stands and morning teas. It has never and will never accept federal government funding. But today the ASRC has thousands of supporters giving what they can and it is now in a position to support projects and initiatives that build capacity and fund refugee-led organisations across Australia and the Asia-Pacific.

Joining the movement of compassion and justice were volunteers who knew we could and must do better; they were there to welcome and support people who needed the ASRC. Starting as a handful of people armed with paint brushes, tins of food and a smile in 2001, the volunteer base has grown to more than 1200 people each year who make what the ASRC does possible.

I have volunteered on reception since January 2002. During these nineteen-and-a-half years, I have received far more than I have given. There have been many injustices but there have always been people who stood up against them successfully. We've had many challenges through the years, but somehow the organisation always rises in a way that doesn't compromise the fundamental core value of respecting all human rights. We are not perfect but I have never seen us compromise on these values. And that's why over the years we've grown from a handful of volunteers to thousands who believe in the ASRC's mission and the people we serve.

Joan, volunteer since 2002

In 2020, as the ASRC was looking to the future, the COVID-19 pandemic hit, and the Centre changed its ways of working to respond to people's new and emerging needs. The ASRC saw a three-fold increase in service demand almost overnight. With no access to government subsidies or recovery programs, people seeking asylum were among the most vulnerable in this once-in-a-hundred-year event.

But there was still hope amid the adversity: as part of its COVID-19 response, in 2020 the ASRC was able to employ 105 people full-time who were accessing its services, centering their rights and their voices. This is the ASRC's future.

Today, the ASRC continues to be powered by hope. And by its values. To be fearless and relentless in the pursuit of justice, always independent, filling gaps in policy through service and centring the voices and upholding the rights of people seeking asylum.

It has grown from a humble TAFE class to encompass thousands of volunteers and hundreds of thousands of supporters in a powerful movement, powered by the strength, resilience and stories of more than twenty-thousand people seeking asylum.

My dream is that fifty years from now we have not built tougher borders or higher walls to stop human beings finding safety and freedom but a longer table with a seat for everyone. We have met the challenge of climate change and avoided creating future generations of refugees. And we have a global community where refugees are welcomed with open arms and provided with protection, safety and opportunity, simply for being human. I hope we no longer follow the drumbeat of racism and fear that betrays our hearts and moral compass and awaken the best of us, an Us that sees and affirms what unites us, celebrates our beautiful differences and believes we are all equal, we all matter and we must all be free and safe to have a society worth being part of and proud of.

Kon Karapanagiotidis,
founder and CEO

Acknowledgements

A project this monumental can only be realised with equally monumental generosity.

Foremost, this book is indebted to the twenty-four contributors who shared their stories. Thank you for your time, energy and generosity. It is an act of immense bravery to publicly share your experiences. We acknowledge that for many contributors this experience was complicated by trauma both past and ongoing. You owe Australia nothing and have given so much. Thank you.

To Liliana Maria Sanchez Cornejo and Abdul Karim Hekmat, thank you for drawing on your lived experiences and academic expertise to highlight the importance of storytelling and bearing witness.

To the selection committee, Liliana Maria Sanchez Cornejo and Ogy Simic, thank you for your invaluable guidance, insight and integrity in developing the book. Thank you for your dedication to ensuring this book represents the diverse identities and stories of people with lived experience of seeking asylum.

Thank you, Black Inc., for supporting the conceptualisation, planning and development of *Seeking Asylum* and providing your expert services gratis. Every step of the way, your team has held this project to an uncompromising standard and the highest integrity. Thank you, in particular, to Kirstie Innes-Will for assiduously editing each word with a careful hand; to Tristan Main, for designing the cover and internal pages with sincere reverence; to Caitlin Yates, for taking our idea and turning it into a book that will sit proudly on shelves across the nation.

To Aesop and the Aesop Foundation, your generous support has enabled this book to be created without compromise. We thank you for your ongoing commitment to amplifying the voices of people with lived experience of seeking asylum.

Thank you to Julian Burnside and Jana Favero, for concisely distilling the mud of immigration politics, and to Kon Karapanagiotidis, for your words of hope. To Allison Fogarty, Chloe Adams and Amelia Willis, for writing up several of the pieces. And to Lilith Fraser, for tackling the tasks that daunted others.

To Kate Disher-Quill, the creator of *Earshot: A Photographic Collection of Stories on Deafness and Hearing Loss*, Arrielle Gamble and Daniel New for your encouragement and advice when this book was just an idea, thank you.

Thank you to the ASRC team for championing allyship and helping bring *Seeking Asylum* to the bookshelves of everyday Australians. To Katrina Grant, for your expert guidance in making every effort meaningful, and to Alan White for your leadership in laying the foundations of the book and guiding its development. And to Sam Biddle, for your humble, deep and unbridled commitment to supporting people in bringing their own stories to life: you did so with dignity, respect and care, curating an immersive photographic representation of the heart of the book, its people.

———

Black Inc. and the ASRC are grateful for the support of the following organisations

Penguin Random House
United Book Distributors
Booktopia
Dymocks Booksellers
Kinokuniya
Abbey's Bookshop
Readings Books & Music
Gleebooks
Fullers Bookshop
Imprints Booksellers
Avid Reader
Riverbend Books
Boffins Books
Paperchain Bookstore
Booksellers' Choice Group
Neighbourhood Books
Brunswick Bound
The Leaf Bookshop
Leading Edge Group
Better Reading

As *Seeking Asylum: Our Stories* lands on bookshelves across Australia, it leaves a lasting legacy, with 100 per cent of net proceeds dedicated to funding projects that support refugee-led initiatives or that build people's capacity to tell their story in their own way, where they can choose how and when their voice is amplified.

One area of investment will continue to be the ASRC's Community Advocacy and Power Program, a three-month intensive training program to equip people with lived experience with the leadership and storytelling skills they desire to become powerful advocates for the refugee community. Since its inception in 2016, this program has seen more than 150 people graduate, and it is now run across Australia.

During the curation process for *Seeking Asylum*, contributors were remunerated for the time they have given to making this book possible. At all times, contributors have had the ability to withdraw consent and have had editorial purview over their story and their image.

Five Ways to Support People Seeking Asylum

Listen

By listening to and learning from people with lived experience of seeking asylum, you'll be better equipped as an ally to fight for change. We recommend listening to podcasts, watching films, reading books and following advocates with lived experience on social media. Whenever possible, amplify the voices of people with lived experience before raising your own.

Challenge

We've all heard the quote, 'the only thing necessary for the triumph of evil is for good people to do nothing'. Your voice can challenge the attitudes that permit cruelty. Conversations with friends and family members who hold different views can be challenging, but if we don't speak up there's little chance of change.

Volunteer

Volunteers are the backbone of the Asylum Seeker Resource Centre and many other grassroots refugee organisations. Positions with the ASRC are regularly advertised (asrc.org.au/volunteer) and each role requires a different set of skills, experience and availability, with options to volunteer remotely too. You can also seek out other local refugee organisations who are doing great work and would benefit from your time and compassion.

Donate

There are many organisations working in the refugee sector within Australia, some of which are refugee-led, who would value your support to make their work possible.

The ASRC plays an important role in the sector, both as a partner in advocacy and through critical service delivery, but accepts no federal government funding. This means the ASRC can be an independent voice for justice and hold our leaders to account. As such, the ASRC relies on donations from our community, made up of compassionate individuals, businesses, organisations and larger philanthropic institutions. Every dollar makes a difference in the lives of people seeking asylum.

Advocate

There are many ways to take action – protesting, calling your local MP, signing petitions and raising your voice on social media all help hold the government accountable. For actions you can take right now, see: asrc.org.au/take-action.